PRAISE FOR SUE WILI

How to Survive Death an

Foreword Reviews Indie Book of the Year Award, Gold Star
2021 Clara Johnson Award for Women's Literature, sponsored by Jane's Stories Press Foundation
Literary Hub's Best of the University Presses: One of 100 books to escape the news
One of *Big Other*'s Most Anticipated Small Press Books of 2020
She Reads: One of 11 memoirs by unbreakable women

"The book's title may suggest this is a morbid book; yet, Silverman in her own clever way leans towards tongue-in-cheek, mixing pop culture, literature, and history with her stories and, of course, her unending quest to survive."
—BrevityMag.com

"Self-aware, quirky, and fiercely intelligent. . . . Silverman achieves a kind of immortality. Readers will find both traditionally and experimentally structured essays. Because of the distinctive subject matter and Silverman's vast writing talents, the book will appeal to new and experienced readers alike. . . . Read any random passage from any random page, and your ears will be delighted by a kaleidoscope of sound."
—*Hippocampus Magazine*

"Silverman's fourth memoir is really about coming to terms with physical death while seeking to create immortal work."
—EVETTE DIONNE, *Bitch*

"Silverman's new book is a joyously unconventional memoir written at least in part as a hedge against mortality. It will shake loose memories, invite you to ponder, and, maybe best of all, make you laugh. This is a marvelously written, imaginative, and seriously funny book."
—ABIGAIL THOMAS, *New York Times* best-selling author

"With true originality and wit, Silverman takes readers on a wild ride through time, memory, pleasure, and trauma. What remains is a deeply human portrait of one woman's resilience and the power of her spirit. I couldn't put it down."
—CHRISTINA HAAG, *New York Times* best-selling author

The Pat Boone Fan Club: My Life as a White Anglo-Saxon Jew

"Silverman's language is, by turns, blunt, wrenching, sophisticated, lyrical, tender, and hilarious. She writes with wicked dark humor, splendid intelligence, wry wit, and honest confrontation. There's no other book quite like it."

—LEE MARTIN, author of *From Our House*

"A masterly stylist continues her uncompromising examination of the inner life."

—*Kirkus Reviews*

"Although many of the topics and themes in these essays are somber and sincere, Silverman's ever-present humor sets a self-deprecating tone. . . . Readers will relate to these stories, for while they're directly about this writer's spiritual journey, they're also about the universal feeling that one doesn't quite belong, and the fact that Silverman has survived, recovered, and discovered her true self gives hope to the rest of us."

—NewPages.com

"Silverman is a stunning, unconventional writer of memoirs. The title alone deserves scrutiny (and a prize)."

—*Newworld Review*

"A delightful and humorous memoir. . . . The book surprised me with its humor, irony, and range of voices. The title is a clue to the tone of playfulness and the different shifting lenses through which we'll view her life. Sue seems to delight in the carnival of wavy mirrors in the funhouse to turn 'reality' upside down and backwards as she experiments with language."

—National Association of Memoir Writers

"Silverman's writing is very alive. As a reader you feel immersed in her world, not just seeing it but feeling, tasting and smelling it."

—*New Book Review*

Love Sick: One Woman's Journey through Sexual Addiction

"*Love Sick* provides an honest and deeply chilling account of what it's like to suffer from a compulsion to look for love in what are most definitely all the wrong places."

—FRANCINE PROSE, *Elle*

"A self-proclaimed addict looks unflinchingly at the source of her sickness and her road to recovery."

—*O, The Oprah Magazine*

"Compelling. . . . Silverman explores the psychology of addiction on a deeply personal level. Candid, emotionally raw . . . never sugarcoated. . . . Deeply moving."

—*Booklist*

"Thanks in large part to fearless writers such as Silverman, our culture is confronting the wretched behaviors that exist even in homes with facades of normalcy."

—MARY ANN LINDLEY, *Tallahassee Democrat*

"In the existing literature on sexual addiction, this book stands alone: a woman's narrative of her own personal story. As self-help, *Love Sick* will resonate with not only those who suffer from sexual addiction, but also anyone whose compulsive behavior, whether with drugs, money, or food, threatens his or her emotional well-being. And as memoir, Silverman's account is an important literary accomplishment, one that will move anyone who reads it."

—recoveryworld.com

"Silverman's stark story of struggle and recovery, told without jargon or psychobabble, creates a wrenching portrait many women will relate to—a portrait of someone who is looking for love, but finds sex instead."

—*Lifetime*

"Silverman is a wonderful writer. With her searing honesty, sharp perceptions, and ability to convey the nuances of emotional terrain, she sheds light on a topic that has been shrouded in secrecy and muddled in misperceptions."

—DEBORAH TANNEN, *New York Times* best-selling author

Because I Remember Terror, Father, I Remember You

"Beautiful, rocketing prose."
—*Tallahassee Democrat*

"Silverman's lyric style transforms a ravaged childhood into a work of art. The book reads like a poem."
—*St. Petersburg Times*

"A rough emotional ride, but it is well worth it."
—*Ms. Magazine*

"Profoundly moving in its portrait of a child's fear, confusion, and desperate search for a safe place."
—*Kirkus Reviews*

"Searing, brave, powerfully written.... Silverman's memoir is about more than incest: it is about evil, about denial, about the great chasm between the public facade of a prominent, successful family and its painful reality, and it is about how, as in a Greek tragedy, a curse has been passed down through several generations. This book is the cry that shatters that curse."
—ADAM HOCHSCHILD, author of *King Leopold's Ghost: A Story of Greed, Terror, and Heroism in Colonial Africa*

"A terrifying and heartening book. I know it is going to be passed urgently from hand to hand."
—ROSELLEN BROWN, *New York Times* best-selling author

Selected Misdemeanors

Selected
Misdemeanors

Essays *at the* Mercy *of the* Reader

SUE WILLIAM SILVERMAN

University of Nebraska Press   Lincoln

© 2025 by Sue William Silverman

Acknowledgments for the use of previously published material appear on pages 181–82, which constitute an extension of the copyright page.

All photographs are courtesy of the author.

All rights reserved

The University of Nebraska Press is part of a land-grant institution with campuses and programs on the past, present, and future homelands of the Pawnee, Ponca, Otoe-Missouria, Omaha, Dakota, Lakota, Kaw, Cheyenne, and Arapaho Peoples, as well as those of the relocated Ho-Chunk, Sac and Fox, and Iowa Peoples.

♾

For customers in the EU with safety/GPSR concerns, contact: gpsr@mare-nostrum.co.uk
Mare Nostrum Group BV
Mauritskade 21D
1091 GC Amsterdam
The Netherlands

Library of Congress Cataloging-in-Publication Data
Names: Silverman, Sue William author
Title: Selected misdemeanors: essays at the mercy of the reader / Sue William Silverman.
Description: Lincoln: University of Nebraska Press, 2025.
Identifiers: LCCN 2024061903
ISBN 9781496244222 paperback
ISBN 9781496244550 epub
ISBN 9781496244567 pdf
Subjects: BISAC: BIOGRAPHY & AUTOBIOGRAPHY / Women | LITERARY COLLECTIONS / Essays | LCGFT: Essays
Classification: LCC PS3619.I5524 S45 2025 | DDC 814/.6—dc23/eng/20250321
LC record available at https://lccn.loc.gov/2024061903

Designed and set in Minion Pro by L. Welch.

For all my dangerous muses, dead and/or alive, without whom this book would not be possible.

To go wrong in one's own way is better than to go right in someone else's.

—Fyodor Dostoevsky, *Crime and Punishment*

CONTENTS

Author's Note   xiii

Part 1. Strange Entanglements

At the Apollo Theatre   3
Coming Attractions   5
Child Care   10
On Understanding Time for the First Time   11
Miss Demeanor Considers the Time When She Was Forced to Hold the Crayon . . .   12
Scratching the Surface   14
Time Travel for Beginners   18
Postcard: The Berkshires   21
A Treatise on Dark Matter(s)   22
Learning the Antimatter of What Matters   26
Retainer   28
Postcard: Monhegan Island, Maine   29
Harbor Lights   30
Miss Demeanor Considers the Time in Puerto Rico . . .   32
7-Up as a Cure for Irony   34
The Silence Detector   36
My Russian Heritage   44
Drinks for All Occasions   46
Snow on Cherries   49
Love Deferment   51
Miss Demeanor Considers the First of Many Jobs . . .   56
Miss Demeanor Considers the Time She Lived in a Room . . .   58
Respect, Almost   60
Miss Demeanor Considers the Time She Posed as an Israeli . . .   62
Manilow Fidelity   64
Carry On   66

Part 2. How To and How Not

Library with Hyacinth, Girl, and Guns 71

How To 74

How to Find a Snow Leopard in Georgia 76

Negative Capabilities 78

Miss Demeanor Considers the Time She Hid . . . 80

Miss Demeanor Considers the Time She Was Married . . . 82

Mug Shots with Fellow Fugitives 84

The Poetic Sentence 86

Missing the Clues 90

On Liminality 91

Exchange Rates 99

Remembrance of Things Past 102

The Long Road Out of Eden 103

Postcard: Greetings from Atlantic City! 105

The Undertaking 106

Reflections on *Blue Velvet* 109

The Family *Chiroptera* 111

The Soft Beauty of an Ordinary Life 115

Miss Demeanor Considers the Time She Stood under the Boardwalk . . . 118

Trashy 120

Miss Demeanor Considers the Time between Hippiedom and Adulthood . . . 122

Degas Paints the Chippendales and Me 124

Part 3. Grieflets

Too 129

Grieflets 130

Psych Ward, Drought 132

Expiration Date 135

Against Ruin 137

Emerald Isle 138

Al Di Là 139

Into the Wild of the Calm 143

The Lost Art of the Near Tilt 144

The Origin of Her Superpowers 146

Miss Demeanor Must Consider, Whether She Wants to or Not . . . 148

Miss Demeanor Must Also Consider the Time Her Father . . . 150

Tinea Capitis 152

A Grand Unified Theory of Disease 155

Organ Music 159

Dyscalculia 163

Postcard: The Big Apple! 166

Postcard: New York City 167

Xeroxing Christie 168

Miss Demeanor Considers the Time She Got Her First Author Photo . . . 170

Miss Demeanor Considers Her Desk (Messy Like Her Life) . . . 172

The Memory Box 174

Seeking Paradise on the Road to Nowhere 176

Acknowledgments 181

AUTHOR'S NOTE

Susumu Tonegawa, a Nobel Prize winner in physiology, says that "recalling a memory is not like playing a tape recorder. It's a creative process." This is also a definition of creative nonfiction and reflects how I portray events contained in this book. Others might recall or interpret events differently. I only claim my memories—and how they evolved over the years—as my own metaphoric truth, my own understanding. In short, I give you, dear reader, my most honest testimony.

Selected Misdemeanors

Part 1

Strange Entanglements

> One of the strangest aspects of quantum physics is entanglement: If you observe a particle in one place, another particle—even one light-years away—will instantly change its properties, as if the two are connected by a mysterious communication channel.
> —Gabriel Popkin, *Science*

At the Apollo Theatre

St. Thomas, circa late 1950s

My father sexually misloved me growing up, but that's another story. This story is about Marko the Magnifiko, a magician who wore a turban and silky Turkish pants. No shirt. Gold necklaces. A red bauble dangled from an ear.

He rolled a mahogany barrel to the center of the stage in this movie theater where I usually watched films such as *House of Wax*. But Marko the Magnifiko was real, the main attraction, and *live*. He thumped the barrel to show the children its heft. He scanned the audience seeking an assistant.

I waved my arms knowing, from the outset, *I* had to be chosen, selected over all the other kids. Having recently moved here from DC, where I was born, I already felt drenched in island magic, flowers blossoming in West Indian sun year-round.

And sure enough, there I was on stage!

The barrel lay on its side facing the audience. Marko the Magnifiko helped me on until I sat astride it, like riding one of the island donkeys. He squatted behind it, arms outstretched, his feet firmly planted. With his teeth he lifted it. I heard him straining under the weight. He raised it higher. I felt as if I were levitating . . . up, up, up a volcanic mountain until all of St. Thomas expanded below me. I imagined I saw the bank my father opened when we moved here; our Danish Colonial house atop Blackbeard's Hill; my mother on the verandah painting watercolors; my older sister swimming in Magen's Bay; the Antilles School, where I attended third grade; islanders shopping in Market Square; cruise ships in the harbor; all the blues and greens of the Caribbean Sea.

Then I was blinded by pure light. Not the tropical sun. A spotlight beamed from the ceiling of the Apollo Theatre. The island vanished. I couldn't even see the audience. Nor could I see Marko the Magnifiko shadowed behind me.

In the glare, I was only aware of me, still on the barrel, perpendicular to his body. I barely breathed, didn't move a muscle.

I sat perfectly balanced, six feet up in the air, even knowing Marko the Magnifiko's teeth could pop out at any moment, sending me sprawling in splinters.

Was this real?

Was it worth the risk?

Did I think Marko the Magnifiko could *abracadabra* me into a little girl with a different father?

No.

But there was still magic in levitating, in seeing, and in being seen.

Coming Attractions

I sit on a stool in Caribbean sunlight as a fortune teller asks to see my palm. Her Carnival booth, decorated with seashells, mirrors, and scarves, is in Emancipation Park, crowded with food stands and steel-drum bands. I'm only vaguely aware of the calypso music, the swarm of dancers. The fortune teller, in a red madras dress, sets down her palm-leaf fan. Bending close to me, she traces the lines on my sweating hand as the blue scarves billow in trade winds. Her predictions themselves are soft blossoming promises: *sweet love, sweet marriage, sweet babies*. In fourth grade, I am young enough to believe her foretelling, to believe the story she tells is *my* story.

The Life Line
What the fortune teller doesn't predict is more important than what she does. She does not predict that the movie *Sundays and Cybèle* will upend my life when I'm a college freshman in Boston. The movie depicts a psychologically wounded veteran and a neglected child who engage in an intimate but seemingly nonsexual relationship that goes tragically awry. He is killed by an angry mob. Without him, the girl's slender shoulders bend under the weight of loss. Neither character could foresee that their unsanctioned obsession would destroy them both.

She does not predict that, about the same time I see the movie, I will become obsessed with a man, Forrest, more than twice my age, who lives across the street from my college dorm. She does not predict how, as soon as I return from class, I will sit on my bed, nestled into the bay window, waiting for him to appear. When he does, he waves. I wave back. One day he lifts his blue telephone, a signal he wants my number. I glance around. *Yes*: my roommate's vase of red roses, a gift from her boyfriend. Seven times, I hold up the number of flowers to indicate each digit of the pay phone in the corridor.

When it rings, I race down the hall to answer.

When he asks me my favorite singer, I say the Beatles.

"No, no," he says. His voice is low, urgent. "Sinatra. Listen to Frank Sinatra."

I perch on the stool by the pay phone, a wall of graffiti beside it. With a black pen I print the letter "F": for "Frank," for "Forrest." I draw a rose-petaled heart around it.

Does permanent ink foretell a lasting future?

I no longer care about classes, about grades, about boys my age. I pretend Forrest doesn't have a wife. All I crave is meeting him in his green Mercedes. He takes me out to dinner. He takes me out for sex. He promises love. Autumn nights he drives me back to my dorm in Back Bay, his silvery hair bright with moonlight. Predictably, I don't consider the distance to the moon, the loneliness in Sinatra's voice.

By spring, Forrest disappears. But he never really leaves. He remains in the scent of red roses, in a black graffitied heart. Years later, I still listen to Sinatra. How can this lingering persist for someone I never really knew?

It perseveres because I gaze into the future for another obsession to replace him, and *him*, and *him*.

The Heart Line

The fortune teller does not predict how the title character in the movie *The Story of Adèle H.* will infuse my soul with her obsession. In real life, Adèle H. was Victor Hugo's daughter, and the movie is based on her diaries. I watch the film in a theater in Galveston, Texas, where I live with my first husband, whom I want to leave. Emotionally, he's already left me: he works until late at night, never tells me he loves me. I'm having an affair with a man full of promises who, I predict, will be more loving.

I see Adèle as a heroine who follows the object of her desire, a dashing lieutenant, around the world, even though he rejects her over and over. This lieutenant to whom, in her fantasies, she is married is superficial and callow. Yet neither Adèle on the screen nor I sitting in the theater recognize this. In her diary she writes that she hopes to win him over with her gentleness.

Throughout the movie, Adèle curls up alone in a rumpled bed. She scribbles in her journal. Ink stains her fingers. Darker stains vein her heart. She tries to portray her soulful need on page after page after page. The lieutenant will never see it. Or her.

Despite evidence to the contrary, I believe her obsession is love. It will be years before I see she did not exhale the misty breath of desire but rather the smoke of ruin. Years before I understand that spending the rest of her days in a mental institution—the result of her obsession—is not romantic.

My Review: 5 Stars
Not sure if the movie motivated me—not sure I needed much motivation—but after I saw it, there I was chasing after this poet, M. I followed him from one writers' conference to another, of all things. Okay, he invited me. And he promised to marry me if I had sex with him. I believed him! I was smitten by the way he draped his jacket over one shoulder, how he focused just on me when he was up at the mic reading his verse. He lived in NYC with his wife. I lived in Texas with my husband. So, between conferences, we wrote letters. I mean there I was lying in bed like Adèle H. pouring my heart out. Until, one day, his letters stopped.
Similarities? You be the judge.
Oh, great acting and direction!

The Head Line

The fortune teller does not predict that Pomme, the protagonist in *The Lacemaker* (titled after a painting by Vermeer), will be another heroine who grasps my hand, twining her fingers with mine. Surely it is *her* hand, her delicate fingers, I hold in the theater in Houston after realizing my second marriage, to an English professor, is also a mistake, despite my prophecy.

Pomme, a shy young woman with pale lips who works in a hair salon, meets Françoise, a student from a wealthy family, unlike her own. She doesn't understand the intellectual discussions among his friends. Françoise wants to "improve" her, believing she deserves a better job than at a salon.

At an unfortunate soiree with Françoise's intellectual friends, she fails to understand the word "dialectic." Pomme further withdraws. She lives a solitary life in a mental institution. It's the only place, the only way, she can survive. Her fingers are diaphanous as lace. Out in the world, skin becomes ripped, ravaged. Lace: her gaze is unable to see through it, while seeing all too well.

The fortune teller does not predict I will never know what "dialectic" means, either.

My Review: 5 Stars

I really get this movie. Who cares about the meaning of "dialectic"? Just for the record, I don't understand the word "phenomenology" either, the subject of my second husband's dissertation. This angers him. He mocks my lack of intellect. But I don't care to know about phenomenology. I thought I'd loved his mind only to discover that's not the kind of knowledge I seek.

Besides, I'm already trailing after another man. I can live without dialectical phenomenology. Like Pomme, it's obsession I can't live without.

Also for the record: I prefer dubbed-in dialogue to reading captions. I like the disconnect between the mouth and the words coming out of it. It's exactly like a faithless lover.

A Psychological Prediction

How could the fortune teller have failed to predict I'd only be married three months before I begin an affair with an orthopedic surgeon who mends broken bones? I had thought, once married, desire for other men would be sutured shut. But marriage isn't encompassing. Isn't enough. I need more. And more.

How to stop this compulsion?

I begin therapy. I sit on the couch in my therapist's blue office. It's quiet as a womb, only a low *thrumming*. A secret message? I study him as if for clues to my future. He leans back in his chair, perfectly balanced, his hands clasped behind his head. Frequently, when he asks a question, he raises an eyebrow. I begin to raise a questioning eyebrow, too.

The therapist explains that "cognitive dissonance is a state of having inconsistent thoughts, beliefs, or attitudes." Based on the movies I inhabit, I believe, at the time, this is a condition experienced only by women. I/we pursue what we call "love" with men capable of emotionally devastating me/us. Even when we foresee the oncoming crack-up, we're unable to avoid it.

Cognitive dissonance: my belief that obsession equals love.

Nights, I lie in bed fantasizing about the therapist, that secret blue thrumming. I imagine scenarios in which he'll leave his wife and children to run away with me. I drive by his house, stalking him.

The Fate Line

Most of my relationships consist of affairs with married men, or with men old enough to be my father. Can that which appears grotesque, in either fiction or reality, be love? Adèle H. is real, Pomme and Cybèle are fictional—but does it matter when the emotions feel true?

These women's stories seep inside each strand of my hair, deeper, until they fill me. I seek, will want, the captivating desolation of their obsessions.

The fortune teller does not predict I will absorb all their silvery heartbreaks, all their enchanting sorrows.

Child Care

St. Thomas, circa 1958

A boy shows me his penis.
Another boy hurls a sharp knife across the room at his sister. Bad aim, though.
My sister bakes me cream puff pastries for breakfast.
I brush my teeth with my father's shaving cream.
A baby dies in her crib.
My sister spends hours alone with the Anglican priest.
A boy dismembers animals.
I dump mounds of sand in my hair so I can spend hours picking it out, grain by grain.
Our skin crisps in tropical sun: hot, red, dangerous.
I'm run over by a bicyclist and sit dazed, alone in the street, bleeding.
Infected mosquito bites tattoo our legs.
A boy in a parachute is swept out to sea, trade winds blowing in the wrong direction.
The rest of us are swept into the future without any parachute at all.

On Understanding Time for the First Time

At dusk, I lean my elbows on the whitewashed rail of the verandah on our house atop Blackbeard's Hill overlooking Charlotte Amalie. Bats paint the air with winged shadows. Lights dotting the downtown, the ships in the harbor, the volcanic mountains resemble a pointillist canvas. The scent of hibiscus, orchid, and ginger flowers rises up from denseness. A rustle of palm fronds. A whirring disturbance in the underbrush. The warmth of sun fades to the coolness of the moon. It will always be this way, yet will never be this way again.

Miss Demeanor Considers the Time When She Was Forced to Hold the Crayon in Her Right Hand for Her Second-Grade School Photo—and Smile the Smile That Launched a Thousand Left-Handed Misunderstandings

Dress, lime green.
Bangs, crooked.
An undershirt peeking out fails to keep her warm.

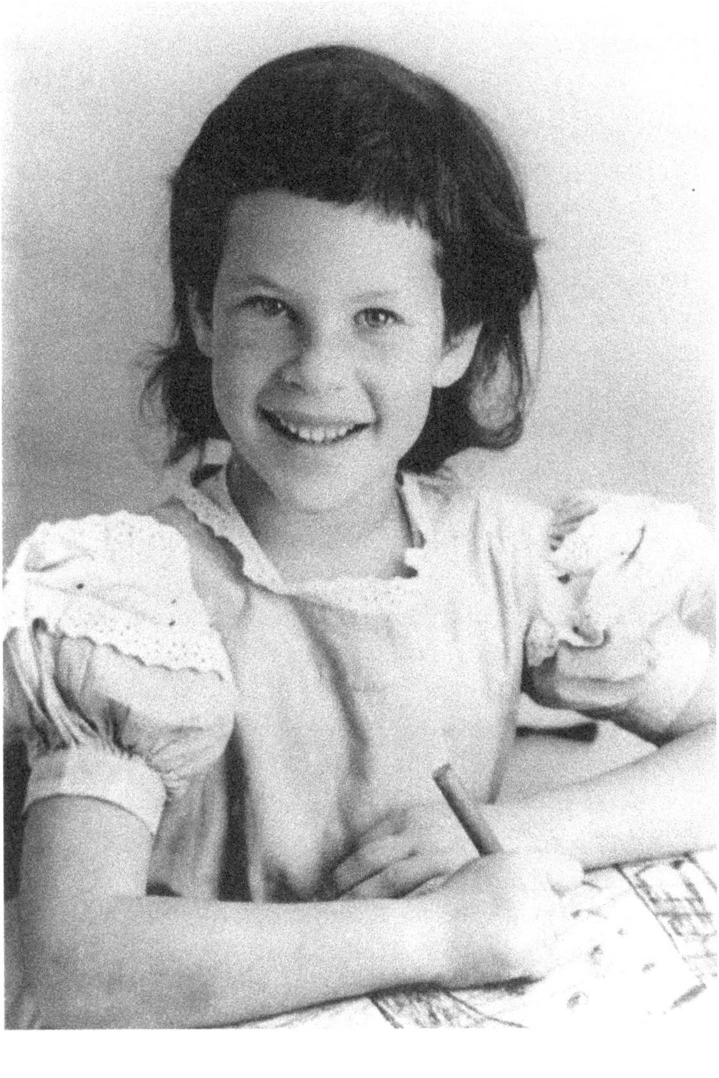

Scratching the Surface

My metal roller skates *clack-clack* the sidewalk of my suburban neighborhood in Bethesda, Maryland. I'm windy-free, this first summer day after first grade. I sweep past the new ranch houses hoping to catch a reflected sight of myself in the large plate-glass windows. My skate key dangles from a frayed blue ribbon around my neck.

I spot a shiny object on the pavement. A dime? Foil from a chewing gum wrapper? I stop. Too fast. I tumble. Scrape my knee. A rivulet of blood trails down my leg. Sitting on the ground, I inspect the wound. A vague awareness of skin, its purpose, seeps into my consciousness. If you peer into a slit of it, you enter a portal, a passageway into an entirely different universe from the one you see around you. A cosmos lives beneath your skin.

I loosen my skates with the key, slip them off, and walk home. I'm so stunned by my newfound knowledge I don't cry.

My mother, a housewife, her hair short, spiky, bristling, accuses me of skating too fast *after I warned you*. She yanks me into the bathroom.

I don't reveal my discovery, certain she wouldn't understand.

I sit on the rim of the tub as she harshly scrubs my knee with soapy water. "Don't be careless," she says.

With a stoppered wand of mercurochrome, she dabs the wound. Mesmerized by the word "mercurochrome," I barely feel the sting. The four syllables roll around my tongue until I taste their curative shade of blood. The wand circles my kneecap, marking the entranceway inside the heretofore unknown *me*.

That evening, when my father, a government official in the Truman administration, returns home from work, he finds me sitting on the floor in my bedroom. I'm combing the hair of my Ginger doll. He kisses my knee with his needy lips. He trails his hand up my leg. After, the wound feels denser, more damaged, deeper below the surface.

I tuck my doll in her box underneath my bed, hidden.

Now, my mother leaves the bathroom, the bottle still on the sink. I'm too young to understand the words on the label.

Only later, I read the ingredients: "½ fluid ounce Dibromoxy Mercury Fluorescein Sodium 2% aqueous solution."

Only later, I read the usage and availability: "General Antiseptic for First Aid distributed by Peoples Drug Stores, Washington, DC."

Only later, I discover its color is carmine, a word I never hear growing up.

Later, I understand secrets encased in chemistry, the medicinal powers hidden within science. Also later, I comprehend the obscure alchemy when you mix seemingly random letters together to form words, and that embedded in each is a distinct meaning, or meanings. Such as the four letters that compose the word "love." When my father says "love" it means one thing; when my favorite uncle tells me he loves me it means something else entirely.

Alone, I close the bathroom door. Fully clothed, I lie flat in the empty bathtub, a container to embrace all of me—what is seen on the outside as well as on the inside—a vessel to encompass my nascent thoughts. I hold the glass bottle toward the window. Light reveals the purple-red color, the properties of magic. It glows with an inner warmth as if it's the nerve center for healing, for secret knowledge. I un-stopper the top. I inhale the scent of crushed rubies.

Here, all seems known as well as protected.

I add another layer of mercurochrome to the scratch. The glass wand cools the hurt while the antiseptic stings it. I love both profound sensations on otherwise ordinary skin.

I also paint an extra flourish of color—a curlicue at the bottom of the injury, an oblong shape encasing it. Despite baths, the color adheres for weeks. Over time it fades, its own form of now-you-see-it-now-you-don't wizardry.

Next year, when we move to St. Thomas, I will see this color in tropical flowers, will compare the magic of never-ending Caribbean summers to this moment of legerdemain.

Back in kindergarten, I sat at a desk with a piece of white construction paper and a handful of crayons. I filled the paper with blocks of blue, red, orange, green, pink, purple. Next, I used a black crayon to scribble over the other colors: a palimpsest the enticing scent of wax. Then, with a toothpick, I carefully scraped at the top layer, forming swirls, stars, triangles, circles until the design revealed snippets of the blue-red-orange-green-pink-purple suddenness below the surface.
    The left side of my palm, where I pressed the drawing while I worked, was also smudged with color—as were my fingertips when I cleaned the toothpick—as if I were part of the overall design.

Maybe I never saw a shiny silver object on the sidewalk in the first place. Only now, still lying alone in the empty bathtub, I realize, whatever it was, I never picked it up. Maybe I let myself fall solely to allow the mystery of my interior body, the hidden world within worlds, to reveal itself.

What would I see if I scratched the surface of my mother and father? Would other parents appear?

When my father was a young boy a dog bit his calf leaving an L-shaped scar. Did his mother dab mercurochrome on it? Did it require stitches? What else punctured his body in addition to the dog's teeth? Was the wound deep enough for anger, rage, loss to slip into his bloodstream, tainting it forever?

Scratches, bites, wounds, then, not only reveal an interior world; they are a portal for humours—sanguine, melancholic, choleric, phlegmatic—to enter and irredeemably transform one's soul.

My soul?

I use mercurochrome for decades until it's banned on October 19, 1998, for containing mercury, discovered to be toxic.

Mercury: the god of travelers, luck, trickery, thieves, as well as the guide to the underworld.

Chrome: healing silver bullets embedded in purple-red ointment.

Together, they repair, or transform, an enigmatic wounded kingdom beneath the membrane of skin—or so I believe.

Time Travel for Beginners

The blonde teen girl dives into the turquoise swimming pool of The Lodge at Smugglers Notch in Vermont. Her slender body barely causes a splash. Afternoons, I watch for her as if I'm on a secret patrol mission. As if stalking her is the sole reason for this family vacation from our home in New Jersey, where we move after leaving St. Thomas, when I enter seventh grade. The image of the girl (by now an elderly woman) is imprisoned in my memory. She is all I recall about this trip with my parents and older sister. Her presence is both ephemeral and indelible, like a paradoxical ghost.

I, now middle-aged myself, don't remember the girl's first name, though I know, with certainty, her last name is "Cushman."

So I'll call her "C."

After C dives into the pool, I slide in after her. I hold onto the ledge as she torpedoes the pool's length. Ripples of displaced water lap my legs. She rockets to the surface. She wipes her face, glancing around, sure everyone at the lodge waits to see her again. In fact, I'm not the only one watching, only the most fervent. C swims to the edge. In one fluid movement, her strong, graceful arms lift her out. She sits in her pink bikini, her legs dangling in the water. I lurk across from her pretending to watch a distant mountain looming over her tanned shoulders. She never notices me. I am too short, my hair too frizzy, too pre-teen, mix-matched and messy. I don't, well, *glow*.

Boys immediately surround C as she shakes water from her hair, now slicked back from her forehead. They pull her to her feet. They jokingly jostle her, excuses to touch her. They hoist her and, laughing, toss her into the pool.

The damp spot on the cement, from where she sat in her wet suit, slowly evaporates.

This is as close to her as I get.

The boys would never—will never—jostle or toss me into the pool.

Afternoons, I imagine, she smells like lemons and honeysuckle, a flirty teenage scent, both serious and not.

Who did she grow up to be? Did her perfection follow her through life?

After dinner, I slip from the room I share with my sister. I follow C, who is with one of the boys, along dimly lit pathways of the resort: past the pool, a gazebo, the deserted ski lift.

C wears a miniskirt and sandals. Her hair billows to her waist. Her night scent is of moist ferns and of sparkling particles swirled to the earth from stars.

The boy nudges her into shadows.

I should return to my own room. Leave. I don't. I can't.

He unbuttons her blouse. He tugs it off her shoulders. Their breaths rush. I hold mine. His hands awkwardly touch her. They kiss. Her mouth tastes like sweet plummy plums. His crew cut brushes her skin. She laughs, a girlish giggle. They sink onto slick grass. He tugs up her skirt. White underwear. Lightheaded, I, too, sprawl on the grass, out of sight.

Not that they'd notice me. I'm too elemental: dirt under my fingernails, knotty hair, sweat that smells earthy.

She is the kind of girl whose lipstick never smudges even after she kisses. Her hair won't be messy when he walks her back to her room. All remains in place because even as the boys touch her, no one will ever really *touch* her. Disturb her. She is the one to distract and unsettle.

Later, the breeze, the scent of emotional disarray, humid and dense, trails me when I return to my cooling white sheets in a distant room in the lodge.

That summer, I would accept any future loss or tragedy if only I could contain all that beauty, power, and perfection for one evening.

Really, I don't, *can't*, imagine C as an old woman. She remains still—and still in that place—futureless. As if time smuggles her away, she is someone who could never be real or true. Yet she's fully alive in memory, the sun always dazzling her blondness in the turquoise pool, the Milky Way swirling it at night.

POSTCARD   *The Berkshires*   PLACE
                                                 STAMP
                                                 HERE

Dear Future Me,

I sit on the shore of a lake. A small breeze ruffles the skin of water as I watch a baby bird, fallen from his nest, unable to fly, float farther and farther from shore.

Love,
Sue

A Treatise on Dark Matter(s)

"D" in ninth-grade science, and I stare out the open window of the summer school classroom in Glen Rock, New Jersey. Boys shoot hoops. What would happen if the basketball continued up, up into the sky, a wayward sun, drenching the playground in light?

Two girls sit on the grass not quite watching the boys, quick glances, while whispering to each other, quiet gossip. I pretend I can hear them, can eavesdrop on any conversation no matter how far away.

A man walks by on the sidewalk, his collie on a leash. I imagine they're searching for someone missing.

In the house across the street, shades are drawn in the upstairs windows. What's happening behind the shades, or down the block, or around the corner?

Dark matter comprises 85 percent of the mass in the universe, yet remains undetectable by scientific equipment, the teacher does not say.

Across the aisle, a boy with brown hair takes notes. A rash patterns his neck. Did an incurable disease cause it?

The girl in front of me wears a checked shift dress. Why did she select that dress to wear this morning? Do we have free will? Or none?

My friends are swimming at the community pool. What songs are they listening to on the transistor? Surely, I sense a vibration, feel music traveling through air, from one destination to another.

What does my mother do alone, every day, in our immaculate brick ranch house with gold wall-to-wall carpet, with the distinct lines of our modern Danish furniture, each bedroom with neatly made beds? Maybe she dusts the raspberry-colored tea service my father brought from Asia. Maybe she straightens crystal glasses and bottles of Grand Marnier, Drambuie, crème de menthe. Maybe she spends hours arranging hors d'oeuvres for my father's important business guests. When she gazes out the window does she beam at our trimmed yard, each blade of grass identical? Tulips, lilacs, and hydrangeas bloom chemically on schedule.

The vein in my summer school teacher's forehead throbs. His lower lids droop. Chalk dust, from where he leaned against the blackboard, smears the back of his blue suit. Am I the only one to notice?

I erase the doodles on my piece of paper. Pink eraser particles dot the page. I scoop them into a pile. Where do they want to go? You can't just throw away precious pink particles.

Some invisible dark matter particles interact with other invisible particles in a way that causes these second particles to not behave like others—via an additional dimension, the teacher does not say.

Once, a boy stabbed me with a pencil. Decades later, the tip remains embedded in my arm. No one ever thought to remove it. Has my skin made peace with it? Is it now part of my molecular structure? Did it *change* my molecular structure? Change me?

That evening, sitting at our round dining room table, I play chess with my father. The overhead light shines on us as if we're trapped together in a spotlight. The white and brown chess pieces are housed in a wooden box. The outside of the box is the actual black-and-white squares of the board. So, when it's open, flat on the table, the two sides of the board are held together by brass hinges, always connected. Over several months, my father endlessly explains rules, strategies, teaching me how to play. I don't pay attention to him, just like I pay no attention in school. Instead, I study the intricately carved features of the chess pieces. I pretend an essence of life resides inside them. Are the pawns secretly jealous of the knights? Is the king angry his fate relies mostly on the movements of the queen? Does the queen relish her power?

Even with a minimum of knowledge, I continue to play chess with my father. His eyebrows lower when he plans strategy, trying to beat me. Even as I ignore strategy, I *sense* where my brown-colored queen or rook or knight or pawn should move. An invisible force guides their quest across the board. Can *I* follow such a quest and vanquish the king?

My father always has the advantage of playing first, with the white pieces, but inequity is also something too elusive, back then, to understand.

Usually when we play, my Scotch terrier, quiet as a shadow, sleeps beside me under the table. His cool nose presses against my foot.

Where do shadows go when they disappear?

After dinner, after my mother fills the dishwasher, she retreats into her bedroom and closes the door.

Once, my mother hacked a snake's head off with a shovel. But that did not prevent sin from entering our criminally perfect garden.

Dark matter remains elusive. From what is it made? Why does it exist in the first place? It's unable to be directly observed: it doesn't absorb, reflect, or emit electromagnetic radiation, the teacher did not say in class earlier today.

From my bed, I watch the moon balancing on the top branch of the evergreen in our yard. Suppose it fizzles out like a defective streetlight? Would I be the only one still able to see?

Even though the Beatles don't yet exist as a band, I'm sure *some* version of the song "Eleanor Rigby" and all the lonely people exist someplace. Somewhere. Even if in the farthest reaches of the universe.

I'm not a quiet child, but I never say what I mean. I'm unable to explain what I mean. I only want to know the unknown. Because the known *is* unknown? Like my parents. Factual information is not what I seek, not what seems important. It's the mystery beneath the surface of skin, or a decibel beneath hearing, I want to claim.

One thing I know: even if I win at chess, my father's queen will always, in this dimension or another, darkly annihilate my king anyway.

Notes

For this essay, I quoted information about dark matter that appears in the article "Scientists Say Dark Matter Could Be Hiding Inside an Extra Dimension," located on the website The Byte, https://futurism.com/the-byte/scientists-say-dark-matter-could-be-hiding-inside-an-extra-dimension, accessed June 11, 2021.

Learning the Antimatter of What Matters

1.

I'm daydreaming through eleventh-grade physics until I hear the term "antimatter." It's the first term or word I've ever heard that seems to describe me. Given that my mind is stuffed with antimatter, I'm of course unable to follow the teacher's explanation. But a non- or anti-explanation is fine. *I am composed of antimatter*, I write in my notebook. I draw a heart around the sentence. How else to explain my anti-interest in every subject in school and my anti-ability to listen?

2.

Although I love ballet, I'm no more proficient at it than I am in physics. While I'm an okay rock 'n' roll dancer, my antimatter body can't control itself for the strict discipline of pirouettes, grand jetés, or arabesques. I'm an anti-particle—the wood floor the particle—and at point of contact, I disappear into heavy anti-helium.

3.

To read, I scrunch in an easy chair in our ranch house, my legs slung over the armrest. I evaporate into pure antimatter for hours. All the novels I read consume me, yet neither my parents nor my sister, who might walk past, can see pure annihilation occurring.

4.

When my boyfriend Jamie and I kiss, I want to ask if he can feel my antimatter lips, the cosmic-ray collision of our mouths.

5.

In tenth grade, I visit a doctor to have a lump removed from under my arm. My mother constantly worries about cancer, and because she worries about it, so do I. I imagine radiation zapping my unhealthy matter into healthy antimatter. The lump, as it turns out, is a benign cyst, perhaps caused by clogged sweat glands, an anti-worry.

6.

A few years later, I once again take physics, this time as a college freshman in Boston. I wait for the professor to explain antimatter, but maybe I'm daydreaming when he does. He's young and good-looking, so I visit him during office hours. He informs me I did not do well on the quiz. Can he privately tutor me in the finer points of antimatter? This is, of course, an anti-question.

7.

As my physics professor slides his hand under my green-plaid miniskirt, I feel a gamma-ray electrical charge that makes me question whether I'm composed of antimatter after all. When he bends close to me, his military-style buzz cut scratches my face. An indentation mars his forehead as if something crucial is missing. His hand reaches the least observable, the most mattered, part of my body's universe. I anti-fail the course, but just barely.

Retainer

My twisted tooth twists my mouth, twists my smile, twists my face, twists my head until I don't know if I see myself front, back, or sideways. My tooth twists because I can't wear my retainer at night. It's a molded piece of plastic, wired, designed to straighten teeth, but it fills my mouth with muteness. My words are those I can't speak anyway. The way my father, instead, nightly fills my mouth with his own twisted language of love, a love too untranslatable, with its own urgent verbs—or are they nouns—that will be with me, fucking forever.

POSTCARD   *Monhegan Island, Maine*   PLACE STAMP HERE

Dear Future Me,

Another family vacation to suffer through. Oh, man, I eat a ton of sugar and get sick as a dog. At the Sunday buffet, miles of food, I gorge on petits fours, éclairs, tartlets, meringues, macarons, puff pastries. I pretty much lose it all about an hour later.

Oh, yeah, there's also a cool ice sculpture of a mermaid overlooking the feast.

Sis roams the shore. Dad swims in freezing water. Mom wants to hold us all together, until her dreams melt away.

Love,
Sue

Harbor Lights

Gravel grits my sweaty palms. My older sister and I walk on our hands outside the gate of our house atop Blackbeard's Hill on St. Thomas. The contest is to see who first reaches the mostly ruined Blackbeard's Castle. Once I cross the limestone road, my hands tangle in overgrown weeds and fever grass. My upside-down sister wears khaki shorts and a wrinkled white shirt. I wear red-white-blue checked shorts and a color-coordinated halter top. This tomboy sister of mine is winning, as always. I only agree to her challenge so she'll play with me. Otherwise, she's off someplace as far as the island allows.

My arms tire. I stagger, taking a few wobbly handstands to rebalance. I no longer see my sister, but I hear her ahead rustling the weeds. Sweat runnels (up? down?) my arms to my neck. Although I'm no longer on the road, one palm lands on a sharp sliver of limestone. My arms collapse as my sister reaches the rusty door of the castle.

"I won!" she yells, triumphant, now standing over me. I want to ask her to take my hand, help me stand. I don't because she won't. She either pretends she doesn't love me or really doesn't. There's probably a difference. I look up at her. Her face is lost in a sheen of tropical light. A drop of her sweat lands on me—warm and salty as the sea—yet feels as distant as the horizon.

"I'm going to the marina," she adds, tucking her shirt into the waistband of her shorts.

At the marina she'll climb the rigging of a ship or play on the trampoline. I myself once tried jumping on the trampoline, but it scared me; I was convinced that with one wild tumble, I'd pitch into the Caribbean. She is the one to jump, bounce, run, climb, flee, walk upside-down to outdistance me, leave me behind.

Later that evening, alone, I rest my elbows on the still-warm railing on the verandah. A trace of trade winds cools my sweaty arms. The sea and sky merge into blackness. Lights on ships moored in the harbor, reflecting in the water, are solitary stars tumbled from the sky.

Does she love me or doesn't she?

By the time we are grown, I still won't know.

I will also never know whether our father misloved her, too. *I ask. I ask.*

She remains a light falling (rising?) beyond my wishes, outside my knowledge, beyond my grasp.

Miss Demeanor Considers the Time in Puerto Rico When She Was Surprised to See Ordinary Stateside Daisies Mingled with Explosive Colors of Hibiscus, Flamboyant, Ginger—Even More Surprised Her Sister Allowed Her One Exotic Moment to Sit beside Her, Her Sister, for Once, Motionless, Not Racing Away

    The girl's stare says, *I love you.*
    The sister whispers, *I love you not.*
    Fading, a snapshot.

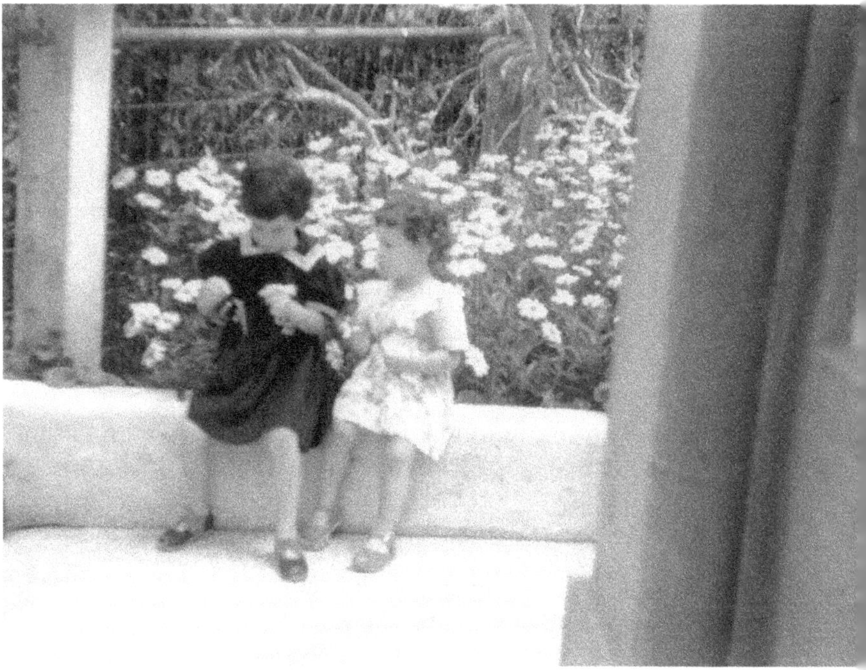

7-Up as a Cure for Irony

I pour a glass of 7-Up before a date with Jamie, my high school boyfriend. Every time. I don't eat dinner. I can't. I tell my parents I'm not hungry. I carry the 7-Up into my bedroom, closing the door. I set the glass on the vanity. I perch on a stool before the oval mirror.

7-Up is honeysuckle summers, the slant of sun at dusk on hydrangeas, the sweetness from an everlasting day that lingers nowhere special.

I switch on my transistor. Here in New Jersey, the radio picks up rock 'n' roll stations in Manhattan. I believe: The third song will predict my future. The fifth song will reveal Jamie's true feelings toward me. What will the seventh song in the line-up portend?

I sip the 7-Up, coolness bubbling my tongue.

Pink lipstick. Eyelash curler. Mascara. It's 6:30 p.m. Jamie will ring the doorbell in half an hour, precisely at 7.

If I ate food, I would feel ill. I almost feel that way even now, sick with longing for a boy who cares for me . . . just not enough.

Doesn't 7-Up provide all the nourishment I need?

I would run away with Jamie. I would marry him. I would have children with him.

He won't do any of these things. He never will. At least not with me.

Besides, I have no real conception of marriage or motherhood. But before these thoughts even rise to the surface of my mind, they evanesce and disappear.

I'm only in tenth grade.

I dab gardenia perfume on my wrists, on the hem of my cotton skirt.

My Scotch terrier bumps the door. I let him in. He plops on the small blue carpet beside my small blue bed. The fur on his back is sculpted like pressed flowers.

If only I could capture a palpable presence of Jamie in one of the songs before it ends. If only I could always see him in the skim of light rippling across the town's turquoise swimming pool. If only his scent remained on the corsages from proms, which decorate my lamp pole, petals now colored rust. If only I could envision him floating, floating, floating in bubblets of 7-Up.

Maybe these are the only places where I'll always ever have him. Jamie.

Jamie is like 7-Up: his blond hair, his pale skin. His fizzy kisses, barely tickling my lips, are too intangible to last, so must be sipped before they flatten.

In winter, walking home from school, I silently wish on early stars just before snowfall.

But now it's summer. When I walk barefoot, the tar on the street almost burns my soles before night cools the heat—like the mercurial temperature of Jamie's love.

Later tonight, after the date with Jamie, I will be back in this room. Alone. I'll open the window. Slide the screen. Watch the effervescent moon for signs that never appear.

The Silence Detector

A body overpowers the light as if it is fiercer, more compelling than the sun. Your skin immediately senses this person is more than a shadow.

~~

This more-than-a-shadow darkens your face and shoulders, creamy-warm with Coppertone. Your towel, on the grass surrounding the public swimming pool, is smooth beneath your bikinied body. You lie on your stomach, head to one side. You open your eyes.

~~

The teenage girl's bikini is skimpier than yours. Her bronze-colored hair, in a French twist, is fastened with a golden barrette. Her features blur in the haze of humid New Jersey. You've never seen her before. Earlier, you heard a rumor: *New girl starting tenth grade!*

~~

Terry, introducing herself, plops on the towel beside you. Her features no longer blur. Rather, they seem expansive. *She* seems expansive, her smile full of energy and movie-star teeth. Bangles glitter her arms. She wears a ruby-red ankle bracelet. She chatters about singing and piano lessons. She dreams of becoming famous.
   She smells like jasmine, cigarette smoke, beer.
   She, like you, is too young to smoke or drink.

~~

Her bare foot grazes your calf. On purpose? A mistake?

You feel dizzy, as if your towel is a magic carpet. You're sailing beyond known horizons.

~~

She glances at you as well as past you, looking around. She stands, stepping off your towel.
You feel stilled, your towel no longer magical.
"Where're the boys?" she asks.
You nod toward the pool. The boys, in a row, climb the ladder up to the diving board. Jamie, your sometime boyfriend, your crush, is about to jump.

~~

Terry watches him leap off the board. As if he is already hers, you can't hear his splash. When he surfaces, she waves at him. You close your eyes.

~~

Several weeks later, walking home from school, you see Terry sitting beside Jamie in the ice cream shop.
The next day, she denies it, or at least claims it a coincidence.

~~

Blinded by her spangled brightness—and that *smile*, that *smile*, that *smile*—you can't yet see where she ends and reality begins.

~~

A friend, sitting beside you in the cafeteria, tells you she saw them together up on the heights, where couples go to kiss.

~~

If only you understood more that day, lying on the towel by the swimming pool, more about love, friendship, loss.

~~

Weeks later, she walks down the corridor at school with another boy.
 Weeks later, she walks down the corridor at school with another other boy.
 Weeks later, she walks down the corridor at school with another other, other boy.

~~

Terry invites you to her house after school. Curious or needy—as if the distinction and distraction of Terry's scent of jasmine-smoke-beer can be yours—you accept.

~~

You sit together on the floor listening to the soundtrack from *West Side Story*. Terry sings along, her voice seemingly as urgent and genuine as the actors on the album.
 Or as false: merely playing a role? Albeit a starring one.

~~

A starring role in *your* life.

~~

After the record ends, Terry stares out the window. Daydreaming of performing on Broadway? She sings in the choir, the Girls' Trio, and plays a lead in the high school production *Best Foot Forward*.

~~

Unlike Terry, you have no dreams of life beyond high school.

~~

You are dreamless.
 You are preoccupied with Jamie. With Terry.

~~

Her much younger sister, maybe only in kindergarten, wanders into the room. She wears cotton shorts and a skimpy t-shirt. Small round burns the size of a cigarette—or miniature suns—trail from her elbow to her wrist. Some seem new. Others are forming scabs.

You inhale quickly.

Terry presses her finger to her lips and whispers, *ssssh*.

~~

Now you wonder: Is Terry's home the only glimpsed truth to mirror the secrets inside your own?

Is that the attraction?

~~

Neither Terry nor her sister seem alarmed. The smile they smile at each other expands then diminishes: the evolution of *smile*.

~~

"Ssssh" is the first word you learned in your own house. Which is both true and not. It, at least, *seems* like the first word you learned in your house, ensuring your house keeps its own secrets silent.

~~

When you see Terry smoking behind the gym after school you think of her sister's arm.

~~

Terry's father has a PhD in chemistry. Before moving to New Jersey, he taught at a university and was head of Phosphor Research at Westinghouse. Now he runs a small business.

~~

Is this a demotion?

Is this why the family flails?

You imagine Terry's father glowing like phosphor, like a cathode-ray tube radiating impurities of light.

~~

Terry's mother wears a satin bathrobe, stained, flecked with ash.

~~

Who presses the cigarette against Terry's sister's arm, you don't think to ask back then.
    Why does the sister's teacher remain silent?
    Reports are never filed with authorities.
    Truth fades like extinguished embers.

~~

Inside other friends' houses, you see no evidence carelessly strewn around. No burns on young girls' arms.
    The air in your own home—*even the air in your own home*—during the day or when friends visit is also pale and pristine. Perfect.

~~

The air in your own home is only caustic as flame at night. The air in your own home only singes when your father stealthily walks down the hallway when the house is supposed to be sleeping.

~~

Ssssh.

~~

Like the fizz of summer-storm lightning, Terry flashes, flirts, sparkles.
    The town, the audience, only witness what they're supposed to.

~~

Yet you see Terry encased in her costume.

No one can touch what surely must be a small round wound blistering her heart.

~~

As graduation nears, you want to rush after her into the world, but inertia weights you to a life with no skills, no talents, no desires, no distant light.
 No Jamie.

~~

After graduation you lose track of her but carry her with you like a secondhand skin.
 She is a residue of loss. An electric scent.

~~

You *wait, wait, wait* to hear Terry singing on the radio.

~~

You only think to search for her on the web years later.
 You discover she died.
 You discover she performed in clubs, hotel bars, cruise ships, on the *Today Show* with Barbara Walters. You watch a video clip of Barbara Walters speaking Terry's name on national television.

~~

But no records. No recording contracts. No fame.

~~

A few blurred, poorly lit YouTube videos are all that remain.

~~

Her voice sounds almost like Judy Garland, almost like Liza Minelli, yearning toward Barbra Streisand.

~~

No singular voice or sound of her own.

~~

No official obituary.

~~

Her father and her mother have obituaries.
 No one wrote one for Terry.

~~

She dimmed from the world in a small whisper.
 She wasn't stronger than the sun. She was ashier.
 Am I the only one left who still hears Terry?

~~

You find no trace of her sister on the web.
 You envision skin puckered and scarred on an arm.

~~

Only now, years after graduation, you acknowledge the alluring, corrupt arc of Terry's smile. Of her family's smiles.

~~

Finally, in the quiet of your own planetary orbit, you acknowledge that the sibilance of Terry's *ssssh* should have broken the silence of your own *ssssh* back in high school.
 It didn't.
 Only now the *ssssh* is spoken aloud.

~~

You hear it.
 A reverberation.

A midnight sun sizzle, a never-ending *ssssh*, a hiss of a cigarette pressed against flesh.

A young girl's skin.

~~

A silence that never stops burning.

My Russian Heritage

My parents, older sister, ancient grandmother, and I hover under the red awning of the Russian Tea Room on Fifty-Seventh Street in Manhattan. A man dressed in a long red Cossack coat and black top hat gestures us through the revolving door. My grandmother glares at him, mumbles under her breath, gives him the evil eye. I am only grateful she doesn't spit three times over her left shoulder to ward off ruin.

Even though I'm young, in seventh grade, the restaurant isn't how I imagined a Russian Tea Room would look based on my grandmother's stories of the Old Country: living in shtetls; the vibration of horse hooves pounding frozen steppes, Cossacks rounding up Jews; the sound of a solitary balalaika drifting across a night the color of ice.

I am surprised my father, also born in Russia, brought my grandmother to a place that recalls the country they fled. But maybe any manifestation of Russia offers comforting familiarity for my grandmother, as opposed to the foreignness, even after all these years, of America. She can't write English. She speaks with a garbled accent. Whenever my sister and I ride our bikes, watch television, wear lipstick, or pull our hair into ponytails she whispers, "Shiksas."

We sit in an elegant red leather banquette with a pink tablecloth. Chandeliers, with dangling red bulbs, illuminate green damask walls, gold samovars, Russian landscape paintings, Fabergé eggs, Matryoshka dolls. Later, when I wander upstairs, I'm dazzled by a stained-glass ceiling and a golden tree sprouting from the lush carpet, glass baubles decorating the branches.

My grandmother wears a bulky black dress, stockings rolled to her knees, shoes bulging from bunions. She smells of damp wool and cabbage. The other patrons, the very American women, wear strings of pearls, diamond earrings, carnelian dinner rings, Hermès scarves, Pucci dresses, and Gucci shoes. Their scents of L'Air du Temps, Shalimar, and Rive Gauche can't possibly smell like the Old Country. The very American men wear silk ties and initialed pocket squares.

The menu offers lobster, herring shuba, caviar, foie gras terrine, vegetable wellington, kulebyaka, côtelette à la Kiev.

Family lore offers stories of trapping and stealing food.

I want to live in the Russian Tea Room, but I want to sit at another table, with another family, not with my grandmother emanating herbs of bitter displacement.

For slurping borscht in the Russian Tea Room, I will never forgive her. For being American, she will never forgive me.

Drinks for All Occasions

Manhattan: rye, vermouth, Angostura bitters, yearning

That late-summer afternoon, New York City sparkled like washed pavement. Sun reflected off asphalt warming façades of brownstone buildings and art deco rooftops. Dreamy, I drifted around Times Square. Lights on Broadway. Bouffant hair. Frosted lipstick. Mary Quant, Yves Saint Laurent, Balmain dresses. Cigarettes in gold monogrammed cases and Roger Vivier pumps with copper buckles. The Peppermint Twist Lounge—all the time hoping that, in a minute, I would no longer be this young teen just off a Greyhound bus from New Jersey. I would be Audrey Hepburn sophisticated, no longer living in the suburbs with my parents.

Dark and Stormy: rum, ginger beer, insistence

The movie *Anatomy of a Murder*, starring Lee Remick, had been filmed about four years earlier. As unlikely as it seemed, when I alighted from that Greyhound bus, I was on my way to meet Lee Remick's brother at the Russian Tea Room. Not that it was a date. It wasn't. My father had a business meeting with him, and I'd begged, pleaded to tag along. Since my dad was already in the city, I was to meet them both at the restaurant.

Boulevardier: bourbon, Campari, sweet vermouth, shyness

Several years later, when I worked for Congressman Ed Koch on Capitol Hill, I was in his New York City office to help with a re-election fundraiser. I had exited at the wrong subway stop, and since I had no idea how to transfer or how to reach my destination, I climbed the steps to the sidewalk. The sunny breeze was a relief from the gritty subway tunnel, but I was still lost. I walked down the sidewalk toward a man and woman, holding hands, to ask directions. I was a few feet away when I realized the man was Dustin Hoffman, star of *The Graduate*. I had been about to inquire how to get to Park Avenue when he smiled at me. Flustered, I rushed off.

Cosmopolitan: vodka, cranberry juice, Cointreau, lime juice, glamour
To meet Lee Remick's brother I had borrowed an outfit from my older sister: a black-and-white sheath with matching bolero jacket. Nylon stockings. Black patent leather pumps. I coiled my hair in a French twist. Luminescent nail polish. Pink, pearly lipstick.

I was equally excited by the prospect of meeting him as I was by the idea of saying to my friends back in New Jersey: *I had drinks at the Russian Tea Room with Lee Remick's brother!*

Daiquiri: white rum, sugar, lime juice, missed opportunity
On another trip to Manhattan, to buy toys at FAO Schwartz for my nephew, I saw the actor Donald Sutherland standing by the entrance. I was particularly startled because, not even a week ago, I'd finished reading the novel *Set This House on Fire* by William Styron, and while reading, I pictured Sutherland as the protagonist. I had even considered sending him a fan letter urging him to buy the film rights and star in the movie.

Now here he was. I paused. He deliberately did not make eye contact with anyone. Why was he simply standing there? If only I had a copy of the novel with me, like a prop I could give him, and which he could make a show of reading.

Moscow Mule: vodka, ginger beer, lime juice (served in copper mug), pretense
When I arrived at the Russian Tea Room, I asked the maître d' for Mr. Remick's table. I sat beside him in a red leather banquette. He was more than a decade older. My father hadn't yet arrived. I can

no longer imagine what we talked about. Did he ask me my favorite subjects in school?

It hardly mattered because I loved the pink tablecloths, the chandeliers with red baubles, the blackberry tea served in clear glass with silver holders. Red caviar. Black.

Finally, how easily I made my entrance onto this set with a full canvas moon. Its painted face was bright with reflected light. I held an unlit cigarette between my fingers. I pretended my tea was wine and asked for more.

Snow on Cherries

1.

On Halloween 2023, snow crowned the bright red fruit still festooned on the tree outside my window. White capping berries resembled a reverse Little Red Riding Hood.

2.

In 1953, Revlon introduced the lipstick and polish "Cherries in the Snow." The first ad featured the model Dorian Leigh, who it's been rumored was the inspiration for Holly Golightly in *Breakfast at Tiffany's*. Perhaps Audrey Hepburn wore this color in the movie, a version that sugar-coated Golightly's fierceness.

3.

Later that decade, I bought this lipstick but never applied it, either lightly or heavily, to my lips. It was smooth, luxurious, almost otherworldly. I marveled at its color when I telescoped it from its golden tube.

4.

Another decade or so later, in a bar not far from Times Square, I sipped cherry brandy. As I drank, I ripped apart cocktail napkins, strewing them across the sticky mahogany in small drifts, or perhaps like stars of some drunken constellation.

5.

After a third glass of the kirsch, I felt dizzy behind my knees. Then my fingertips. My ribs. The base of my throat. The promise of sweetness can fool you like that, if you're not careful.

6.

A man picked me up that night in the bar. My mouth tasted of cool plucked cherries, his the sting of tequila, of salt.

7.

In this version of the tale, the man is the wolf, of course. Unlike other versions, I do not rely upon some fantastical woodsman to rescue me or else perish altogether. In this version, the fruit is not cherry but crabapple, which clings stubbornly to its tree all winter.

Love Deferment

I forever stopped playing my autoharp the evening when I thought no man would ever love me. I was strumming chords to "Puff the Magic Dragon," belting lyrics almost on-key, when the phone rang. I set the instrument on the couch-bed combo in my efficiency apartment off DuPont Circle in DC. Michael. He told me he thought we should stop seeing each other. Which, given the relationship—the *affair*—meant we should stop having sex. Which meant the affair could never, would never evolve into love.

After hanging up the phone, I returned the autoharp to its case and slid it out of sight under the bed.

♪♪♪

My boyfriend at the time, Graham, was away in boot camp training to be a medic in the Army Reserve. What with the draft, it was the best he could do to avoid killing, or being killed, in Vietnam. He'd tried to flunk the physical—something about eating a jar of peanut butter and twenty bananas that might cause a something-or-other temporary ailment. All his attempts to avoid the military failed. He was now stationed at Fort Sam Houston, outside San Antonio, for three months.

Before he left, he asked Michael, his best friend and roommate, to keep an eye on me.

Before he left, I bought the autoharp and a goldfish for company.

Before he left, despite dating four years, he still couldn't, or wouldn't, say he loved me.

♪♪♪

Now, after hanging up with Michael, I slumped against the corduroy bolster pillow. This was my first adult apartment after graduating college, though I couldn't claim to being completely adult. Sure, I earned enough money from my job on Capitol Hill to support myself. But I bought my furniture at the Salvation Army. My waist-long hair was wild and free. I wore bell-bottoms and miniskirts. Love beads encircled my neck. Or perhaps they were un-love beads, a choker.

♪♪♪

The first Saturday in April, after Graham left, Michael and I walked around the Lincoln Memorial and Reflecting Pool. Cherry trees bloomed. We didn't discuss "it" beforehand. Maybe because we were hippies and, well, free love and all that. Or maybe because if Graham couldn't love me, I hoped Michael would. Michael held my hand, pulling me against him, under a tree. His straight brown hair flopped onto his forehead almost covering a small scar intersecting his right eyebrow. I stood on tiptoe to kiss it.

We ate romantic dinners at French bistros in Georgetown or at the restaurant in Dulles Airport that overlooked the runway. We watched planes arrive and depart as if our relationship, too, contained a wider, loving universe.

♪♪♪

Freddy, the goldfish, didn't look healthy from the get-go. He didn't come with instructions, but I sprinkled food into the water after I returned home from work. I watched him listlessly swim around his bowl. I couldn't afford an expensive aquarium. I worried he was bored. Or lonely. But the bowl was too small for a second fish to be his golden soulmate. Sometimes I pressed my face against the glass, so he'd know he wasn't alone. But that seemed to scare him, and he finned away.

♪♪♪

Evenings, after work, after eating a sandwich for dinner, I played the autoharp. I loved pressing my fingers on the chord buttons, the keys clearly labeled. I belted out "This Land Is Your Land" and "If I Had a Hammer." Alone, I played over three hours at a time. Never in front of anyone. Only for myself. And Freddy.

♪♪♪

On the walls of my apartment, I'd hung framed photographs I'd taken with my Nikon. One of the photos was of Graham at National Airport, snapped just before he left for basic training. I stayed with him until he boarded the plane. I hoped that maybe, even moments before he left, he would finally say he loved me. But in the departure lounge, he seemed anxious for the good-byes to be over. I started crying. He held my forearm. "Come on," he said. "Stop crying."

I shook my head. "I can't," I said.

"When I get home . . ." His voice trailed off. He stared past my shoulder unable or unwilling to look at me. He wore a crisp shirt and tie. Unlike me, he didn't dress like a hippie. Maybe he could only love a woman who wore pearls, not plastic love beads, who didn't buy secondhand furniture at the Salvation Army, who played classical music on a violin, not folk songs on an autoharp.

He gave me a quick hug good-bye, so fleeting it felt like emptiness brushing my arms.

Now I looked at him, at his photograph, on my wall. The curls on his head appeared sculpted, each a perfect duplicate of the next. Even in the photo he seemed to be looking past me, not at the lens. I was never sure if he couldn't or wouldn't see me, or if he saw me too well. But if I saw *him* so clearly, why did I even love him—love someone who didn't love me back?

♪♪♪

Weekends I spent with Michael in his apartment, the one he shared with Graham. Graham's bedroom door was always shut. Michael

Love Deferment   53

and I both ignored it. Almost as if Graham had never lived there, as if neither of us knew him.

Periodically I wondered if the affair with Michael was more about revenge. Or maybe I was only lonely. Or maybe I felt most at home in myself when I was making decisions certain to end in disaster.

♪♪♪

In June, I missed my period. I was convinced I was pregnant. This was before *Roe v. Wade*, so abortions were illegal. Felonies. When I told Michael, he turned from me and took a beer from the fridge. I tried to explain I was scared of a baby; I was also scared of a back-alley abortion that might kill me. Michael opened the beer then tossed the bottle top across the room. It pinged the refrigerator and rolled to the floor. "No," he said. "No, no, no."

"No what?" I said.

The oscillating fan blew DC humidity from one side of the kitchen to the other. In its breeze, Michael's bangs drifted up off his forehead. The scar across his eyebrow seemed frailer, as if it, or he, were scared more than angry.

"I'm too young to be a father," he said. "I'm *not* a father."

"Like *I'm* a mother?" I jangled my turquoise-colored wild-child love beads.

I picked up the bottle top and dropped it in the garbage. I opened the apartment door and walked down three flights of stairs to the street.

♪♪♪

A few weeks later, riding home from work on a DC Transit bus, I felt a cramp in my stomach followed by fluid dampening my underwear. When the bus stopped at DuPont Circle, I ran the few blocks to my apartment. My period.

♪♪♪

The following week I received that phone call from Michael. He'd met someone "unattached" is how he phrased it. *He* didn't want to cheat on *her* by continuing to see *me*. But maybe this near-crisis scared him. I never saw him again.

♪♪♪

Not only did I stop playing the autoharp that night, I couldn't or wouldn't even look at it, as much as I once loved it. Yet still I felt it—like a corporeal presence under my bed—when I went to sleep. Finally, I smashed it. I crammed the pieces down the incinerator.

♪♪♪

Around the same time, Freddy died. I found him floating on the top of his fishbowl. I cradled his limp, soggy, orange body but then flushed him down the toilet.

♪♪♪

Evenings, eating dinner alone, I watched the Vietnam War on television: the black-and-white flash of napalm, blood that looked like chocolate syrup in this seemingly nonending war. Certainly, love didn't last nearly as long as the war. Not lasting at all, in fact.

♪♪♪

That night of Michael's phone call, I opened the windows to heavy summer air. To the faint scent of diesel and exhaust from the buses. Voices drifted down the street from DuPont Circle. I can't say my fear that love would always elude me was solely formed in that moment. But for years after, whenever I considered love, *real* love, the images that appeared were of a smudge of blood on my underpants; Graham staring past me; a phone call full of betrayal; an incinerated autoharp; and a lifeless golden fish in a glass bowl, a skim of scum floating on top . . . so many images, like discordant musical notes, deferred, frozen in time.

Miss Demeanor Considers the First of Many Jobs at Which She'll Fail, Not Interested in the Passage of Legislation on Capitol Hill or Much Else, except Meeting Congressmen behind Closed Doors

Eyes downcast posing as earnest.
Forging the name of her congressman.
Yet the bill is hers to pay, not pass.

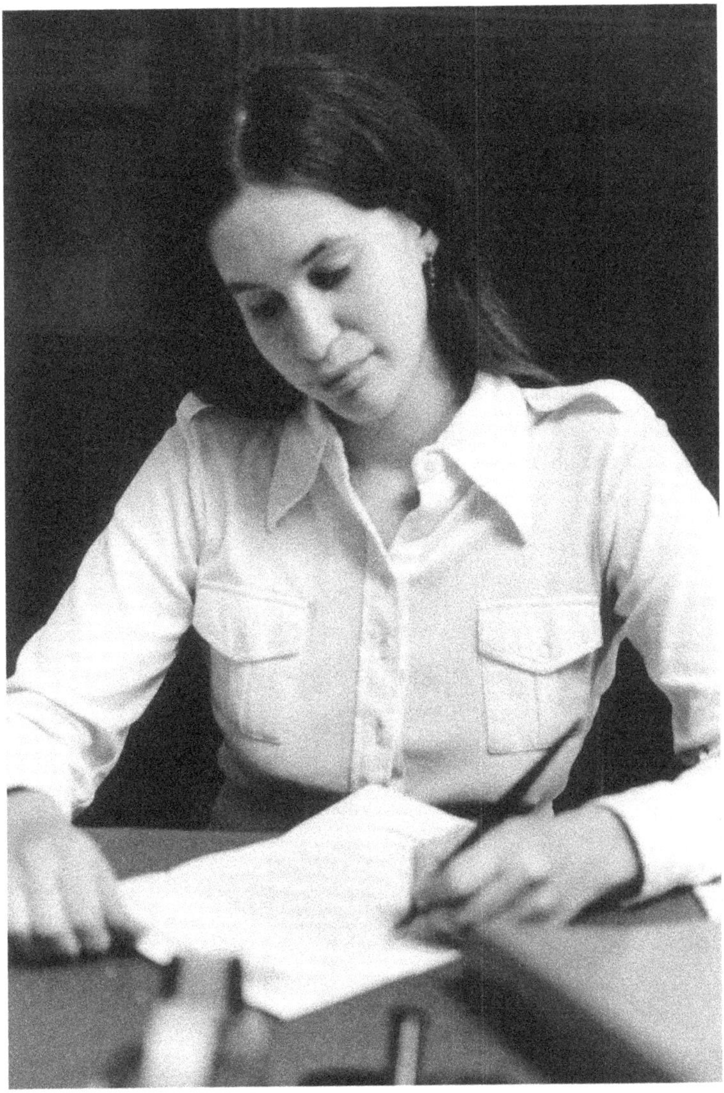

Miss Demeanor Considers the Time She Lived in a Room on a Kibbutz in Israel, in the *Hamsin* Heat of Day, of Night, Mattress Stuffed with Straw, Window Overlooking Donkeys and Apricot Trees, a Partially Written False Letter to Her Lost or Abandoned American Boyfriend, Graham, on a Dusty Table

Furniture, sparse.
Room, barren as her heart.
A sailboat in the desert.

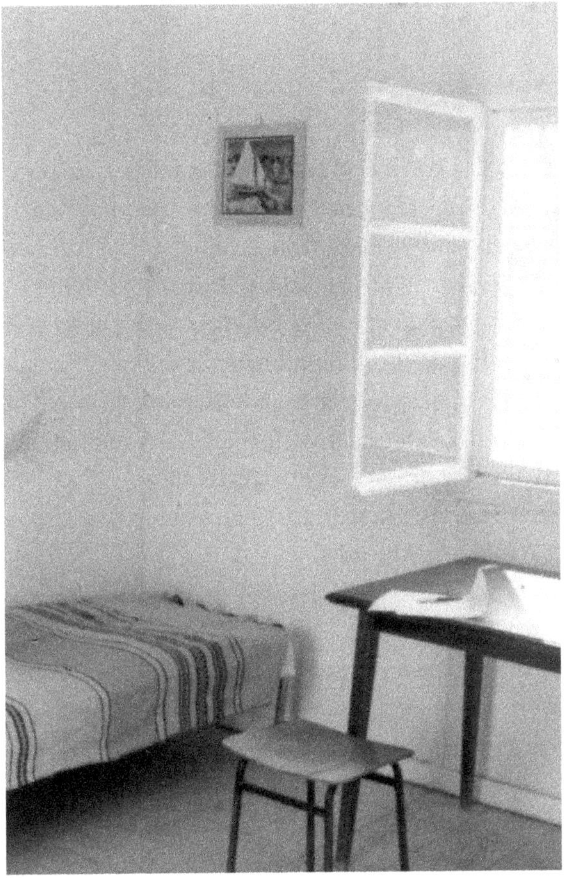

Respect, Almost

After sex, Ari and I lie naked on his thin mattress stuffed with straw. The song "Respect" plays on the radio, a distant version, an echo of lyrics waxing and waning from a radio station barely reaching us from Tel Aviv here in the Galilee. Through the open shutters a breeze, or a suggestion of one, almost cools our sweaty bodies. I lie on my side watching him. Blond hair. Green eyes, though they're closed now. He's a paratrooper, his bungalow on the outer perimeter of the kibbutz, though "outer perimeter" is a misnomer. The entire kibbutz only comprises about thirty structures.

He opens his lids. He whispers the word "respect," shrugging. "What this to mean?" he asks.

He barely speaks English. I know no Hebrew. How to explain such an abstract word?

If I had the vocabulary, I'd explain that "respect" is probably what he doesn't have for me. I'm a loose American girl, wanting to masquerade as an Israeli, spending a few months picking apricots on the kibbutz. He's a tough sabra currently on leave for a few days from the military. When I first met him, I translated blond hair, green eyes, red paratrooper cap, and fearless energy into love. Well, almost love.

I pick up a pencil and print the word on a piece of paper. He flips through a Hebrew-English dictionary.

I glance away, not wanting to see his expression when he understands the word. "Yes, yes, oh," he says, smiling.

Softly, he pushes me back on the mattress that isn't quite a mattress.

Tomorrow, he'll return to the military.

Tomorrow, I will awaken at 4 a.m. to pick apricots.

For years, long after I've left Israel, whenever I hear "Respect," I'll never envision myself. Instead, I'll almost see his blond hair, green eyes, red paratrooper cap and believe it was all almost enough.

Miss Demeanor Considers the Time She Posed as an Israeli, Early Afternoon, in from the Apricot Fields, Not Seeking Her Jewish Roots—In Reality Posing for All the Israeli Boys Who Didn't Speak English, Unsure Why She Was There as She Never Quite Knew Who She Was, What to Say, and with No Language to Say It

American skin, shed.
Israeli skin, tan.
Smile beckoning boys she'll always—yet never—find.

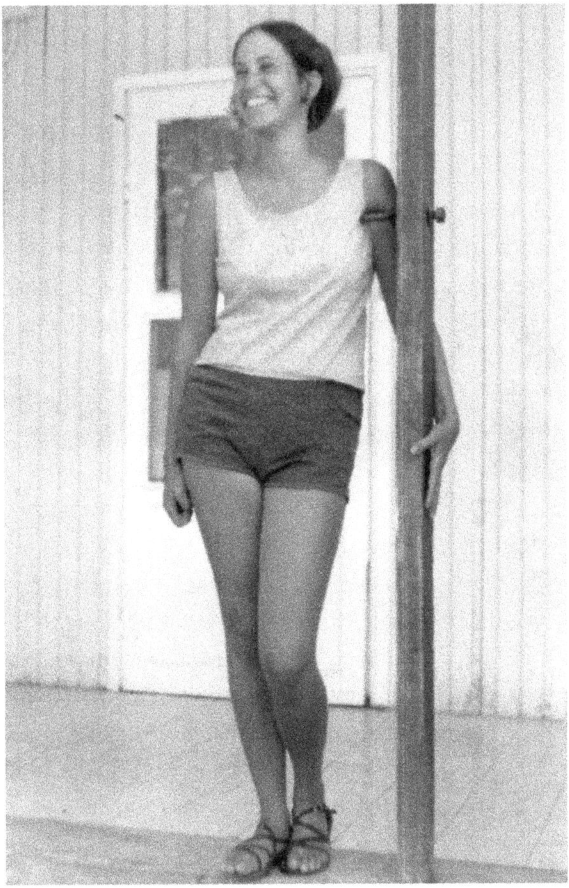

Manilow Fidelity

On a warm evening in Georgia, six women and I sit on folding chairs arranged in a circle. You've seen it—a 12-Step group in a church basement. We are strangers, only connected to each other through Sex and Love Addicts Anonymous. We weep our secrets, spilling them. K wails her love for Barry Manilow, who she claims must be her Higher Power.

Tissues, damp with tears, ripped into shreds or wadded between palms, form shapes resembling clouds. A few months ago, one of my students, from Japan, made me a present of origami in the shape of a star. These paper clouds into which we enfold our tears are a kind of earnest but artless origami.

K exhales more secrets. She drives interstates, looping around Atlanta, listening to Manilow cassettes. With each song all she wants is sex, sex, sex with Manilow. Or someone close enough. A facsimile. She confesses to picking up guys in bars, luring them to her car, cranking the engine, music playing, and she's fucking and blowing to "Can't Smile without You," "Mandy," "Copacabana." *And why can't Barry Manilow be my Higher Power?* she asks, she pleads.

I'm fairly new to recovery, but I'm quite sure this isn't how it works.

Driving home that evening, home, where I live with my second husband, my mind can't stop playing "I Write the Songs." It's on repeat, repeat, repeat. I spin the radio dial seeking Manilow, but no luck. The next day I purchase one of his cassettes. Now, regardless of my husband, I drive around listening, yearning for Barry Manilow. Soon, I know the lyrics and sing along.

This isn't how it's supposed to work . . .

For over a week, I play my cassette virtually nonstop. Then, because *my life has become unmanageable*, I pull the car into a parking lot behind a McDonald's. I stop beside an open dumpster and roll down the window. The scent of hot asphalt, fried grease, and unrequited hunger.

I eject the cassette.

I know what I have to do. Even so, I'll miss the promise of Barry Manilow's sincerity, *can't smile without you . . .*

Is that true?

Stop over-thinking. There is nothing to over-think about Barry Manilow.

I yank the tape from the cassette, unspooling it. I stretch and snap the tape into pieces and toss the entire thing into the dumpster.

Do I need to confess this at the next 12-Step meeting?

How do I find a Higher Power other than Barry Manilow?

The reason why my student crafted an origami sculpture for me is because, given her struggle with English, I'd spent extra hours explaining *Madame Bovary* to her, one of the assigned novels. Throughout, as we read, and I explained, page after page, I felt shame. Is Emma Bovary's reckless behavior, cheating on her husband, different from mine? At least I see solutions other than cyanide! Am I only Emma Bovary "lite"? Kind of like the Easy Listening version? My student would never guess the real "me." She was merely grateful. I was merely mortified.

The star my student made for me is intricately folded, each of its facets a different colored design. One of the common origami folds is a crane, which would have been perfectly (in)appropriate for her to give me, since the crane is monogamous, mating for life. But folding a crane is easy and would have been an ambiguous gift. Take Barry Manilow. His songs are so easy to listen to—smooth, seductive—that you hear them whether you want to or not.

Carry On

After a final visit to my dying parents, I grip my father's hand-carved cane, an art object he bought in Mexico, not one he actually needed. I use it, or pretend to—it won't fit into my suitcase—as I walk the airport concourse toward my plane to Atlanta. People part to make way for me. Kids stare as if waiting for me to crumple to the floor. After I board, the flight attendant solicitously wedges it into an overhead bin. She smiles, pats my arm, and says she'll get it down for me after we land.

On either side of my hair, parted in the middle, I've fastened my mother's two antique hair combs. They are a matching set with tortoise-shell teeth and silver frames. With my thick, heavy hair they're more token than useful.

Yet with these mementos I feel I wear my parents, back to my home, with me.

Even as I know it's not enough.

What I *also* want to carry home with me: their deathbed confessions, words begging forgiveness, profuse apologies for not loving me right. But those words must have faded into ether.

During the flight I fall asleep. I awaken when the wheels touch down. I reach for my hair, streaming across my face. The combs have slipped out, are gone. As travelers stand to depart, I turn to the elderly gentleman sitting behind me. He wears a silk tie and gold cufflinks. I ask if he can search the floor. He holds up his hand, his palm open. He has broken all the teeth of the combs into tiny pieces. Only the silver is intact. A woman, apparently his wife, yells at him, asking why he'd break them?

"I didn't think they belonged to anyone," he says.

"*What?*" I say. "Why would you think *that*?" In a rush I explain about my mother. About saying goodbye to her. About dying.

He doesn't exactly apologize but offers me the pieces. I grab them, some of the tortoise-shell teeth sliding between my fingers. I shove the rest into a pocket.

The flight attendant retrieves the cane.

I want to smack it against the man's head. I want him to feel what I feel.

Instead, I lean forward on the cane, now needing it to hold the weight of my rage. But as quickly as the rage erupted, it dissipates. Slowly, I sway up the aisle, people reaching to steady me. I don't tell them to stop. I am only beginning to feel the burden of preserving the emptiness that remains.

Part 2

How To and How Not

> I was against felonies when a misdemeanor would do.
> —Maggie Stiefvater, *Forever*

Library with Hyacinth, Girl, and Guns

The girl sits behind the circulation desk in the "Arts and Recreation" section, where she's worked nights for over a year. She mainly checks out popular "how to" books for the patrons: how to fix your home, repair your self-esteem, learn a foreign language. Her department is also responsible for overseeing record albums, art reproductions, and prints.

Her favorite books are about how to plant and nurture flowers.

She, herself, does not grow flowers—only knows how to precipitate their ultimate demise.

She traces a finger across slick paper, touching the petals of a hyacinth. Whispers, *hyacinth*.

~~

Later, shelving returned books, she pauses to browse *The Modern Pistol and How to Shoot It* by Walter Winans, an Olympian. She brings it back to her desk. Published in 1919 by G. P. Putnam's Sons, it offers instructions on how to operate pistols from dueling to the fairly new automatic. The not-so-modern book is nearly as old as this Carnegie library, opened in 1911, located in sleepy, dusty Rome, Georgia, more than an hour from Atlanta. She lives here with her second husband, a professor at a local college. He teaches concepts like ekphrasis and phenomenology, which, despite all the books in the library, she doesn't understand.

The girl doesn't own guns any more than she owns flowers. Just as well. With a gun, especially a modern one, ultimate is more ultimate.

~~

According to myth, Apollo, in sadness and grief, created hyacinths from the blood of his lover, Hyacinthus. The god accidentally killed him while playing a game of quoits or discus throwing.

Another version of the myth suggests that a jealous Zephyrus, god of the west wind, also in love with Hyacinthus, deliberately blew the quoit off course to slay him.

Futilely, Apollo tried to save Hyacinthus with ambrosia and herbs.

From the photographs in the book, the girl thinks the blossoms seem fragile, though the bulb is poisonous.

~~

The door to the library is propped open to a slow southern evening scented with betrayal—a subject, she knows, that needs no how to.

~~

Everything is quiet until a man exuding mouthwash and cheap whiskey enters. He asks the girl to play a Johnny Horton song for him. She goes to the shelves of records and locates an album.

The man tries to sing along. But he doesn't know the tune or the lyrics to "Honky-Tonk Man" or "I'm a One-Woman Man." He is missing teeth and garbles the few words he remembers. He seems about to weep. The girl wants to offer him hyacinths. Considers ripping a picture from the book.

The man shuffles off during "The Battle of New Orleans," not knowing, perhaps, how to express his love for Johnny Horton or anything else.

~~

Nine p.m. Closing time.

The girl shelves the hyacinths, guns, myths. The room is still, as books harmoniously settle into their proper niches.

~~

Hyacinths come white, cobalt blue, blood red.
   Guns come steel, automatic, silenced.

~~

Sometimes, sadness is beautiful. In Georgia, for example. On a humid evening. When even lament is sublime.

How To

After abandonment, ritualistically chip off purple glittery nail polish. Stop eating. Or eat too much sugar. Carve slits in skin with razor.
Trim off excess that may remain.
Lie in bed. Stare at ceiling. Stare at water stain in plaster that resembles nothing, not even bad Rorschach.
Observe blood smudge on bed—also not Rorschach.
Check for leaks. Use cloth soaked with cold water and soft brush to clean.
Or don't.
Forget to shower. Forget to change clothes: a tank top and cut-off jeans.
Sleep in clothes.
Afternoons, pull blinds to darken room.
Do not expose to sunlight.
Or open blinds to a swath of sun-harsh sky. Pray it will scorch him/it out of you.
Keep area of operation free of foreign objects. Keep children, pets, and bystanders away from area of operation. Danger indicates an imminently hazardous situation that, if not avoided, will result in death or serious injury.
At night, rites and traditions continuing, stand at the window, palms against panes. Watch planets and stars. Wonder where he is, wonder how this sky contains him and you. If planets and stars were closer, would it be easier to anchor yourself to something other than unknown/known, unfamiliar/familiar locations?
Step back and look from a distance.
Wish night lasted forever.

If night lasted forever . . . How can you not know how to finish that sentence? Swing on a fulcrum of love/hate. Want him back; want to destroy him. Can't sustain one feeling. Don't know how to sustain or cease anything.

That's a lie.

It's self-preservation that's mysterious. Or you don't know how to stop retaliating. It lingers on and on.

After a while—weeks, maybe—leave the house for neon bars. *Select the route that provides the most direct path.*

Blood turns to scotch. Slip into men's beds.

Connect female end of cord to male plug.

Or, better yet, don't.

How to Find a Snow Leopard in Georgia

Wake up in bed at 5 a.m. in rehab to recover from love and sex addiction—with or without a side of drugs.
    Put fuzzy pink-slippered feet on the floor.
    Wiggle your toes in the fuzzy pink slippers.
    Ignore the silence of the room.
    No, pretend the silence of the room is the silence of the icy wilds of Mt. Everest.
    Mt. Everest is the farthest place you can imagine from this room, as you sit on the edge of a bed in a rehab unit in Atlanta.
    You brought *The Snow Leopard* by Peter Matthiessen with you as if it would prepare you for your own expedition. The fact that *this* is the one book you thought to bring to rehab might, in and of itself, be enough proof that you need to be here. Regardless, you now want to be on *his* odyssey, not your own.
    Glancing down at your fuzzy pink-slippered feet, surrounded by gray industrial carpeting, you gaze at a chasm splitting mountain peaks.
    The silence is your own choosing.
    Or isn't.
    All you've ever wanted is a snow leopard to wrap its long tail around you as if the intensity of its stillness could protect you from abandonment, fear, loss, lies. If you, yourself, were a snow leopard, you'd be on an isolated mountaintop where no man could find you. Maybe where you couldn't (don't want to) even find your (somewhat) unknown self. You're sure Mt. Everest's ice is the only scent that soothes you as you watch the circuitous path the snow leopard follows—no one tracking the shallow scuff of your pink slippers.

Wind freezes your senses until all you hear is the sound of distance.

You aren't even sure you exist.

You almost didn't.

Yesterday, you awoke in your bed from too many pills, an accident, but one resulting in numb limbs. You longed for this cold on frozen slopes, following snow leopards to their blessed isolation where no one sees them. No one hunts them.

You don't want to be hunted.

You smell eggs cooking in the base camp cafeteria.

You run your tongue over your teeth as if to sharpen them.

Can you reach the summit?

You taste the silence of white-blue ether. You see a distant spot of fur padding closer. You pad forward on your stealthy pink paws to meet it.

Negative Capabilities

Stand alone in the darkroom.

Open the canister and remove the film.

Find the slit on the edge of the reel and ratchet the spiral of film around the metal cylinder.

Tighter.

Because you are convinced you love your therapist despite magazine articles explaining the difference between "love" and "transference."

Slide to the bottom of the chemical tank.

The film, not you.

He resembles Gregory Peck, whom you've obviously seen only on the screen and in photos.

Turn on the red light.

At this point, you must mix the proper chemicals.

For the film? For you?

Agitate.

Pour out developer.

Halt development with stop bath.

Only film can survive this red bath.

Fill tank with fixer to stabilize film.

Fix and stabilize. *Fix and stabilize!*

The therapist is the same one in that blue office who explained cognitive dissonance when you over-identified with movie heroines.

Outside, humid Galveston, like you, builds toward hurricane-force winds.

Remove from tank and set in cold water.

Rinse.

Sit in your car. Watch him leave his office.

An agent prevents water streaks and bubble marks.

Also, secretly, insert new roll of 35 mm film. Wipe camera lens.

Hang to dry.

Photos. *Only* photos.

The shot: him opening the door of his Mercedes, tossing in his briefcase.

Should you be honest with him or not?

Choose the negative.

Slide into negative carrier.

Place into enlarger.

Enlarge to greatest size possible, up to and including rage. Despair. Unrequited everything.

Project image onto easel.

The shot: him looking at the Gulf over the roof of his car.

Not seeing you.

Turn focus wheel.

Tighter.

Set aperture.

Stop.

Stop!

F-stop.

Insert silver-emulsion paper into easel.

Put paper into chemical tray for sixty seconds until he advances out of white paper, features forming almost as if he's moving toward you, reaching for you, closer, so close now to your face.

The shot: him looking almost like a real person, but not. The way Gregory Peck looks on the silver screen.

Remove with tongs.

The paper, not your heart.

Slide into stop bath for ten seconds to stop his development at the moment he's perfect, under your control.

Miss Demeanor Considers the Time She Hid in a Curtained Photo Booth at a Carnival and Produced a Snapshot That Captured for the First Time the Addict's False Eyes, the Innocently Deceitful Gaze of Her True, Pre-Clinical Self

>Her eyes see you—
>the icy you—
>the ICU.

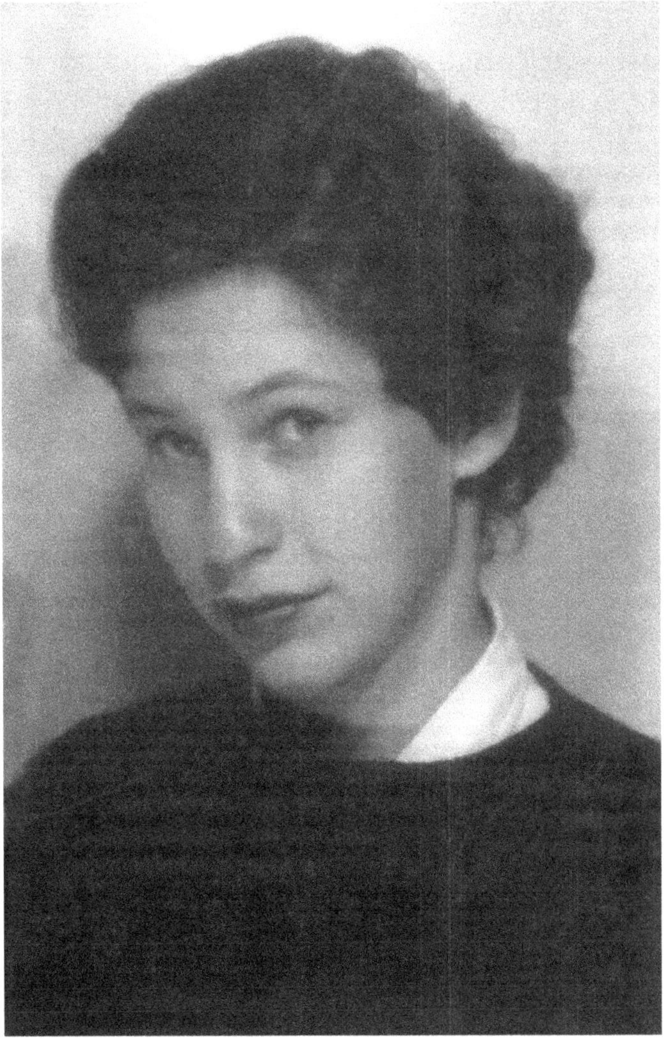

Miss Demeanor Considers the Time She Was Married to Husband #1, Yearning for Another Man Who Didn't Show Up, or Showed Up with Distorted Face, No Longer Wearing the Loving Mask He Wore the Night Before, Requiring Her to Let Go of the Camera and Its Obfuscated Pictures

    Man, gone.
    Lens, shut.
    F-stopped. Or not.

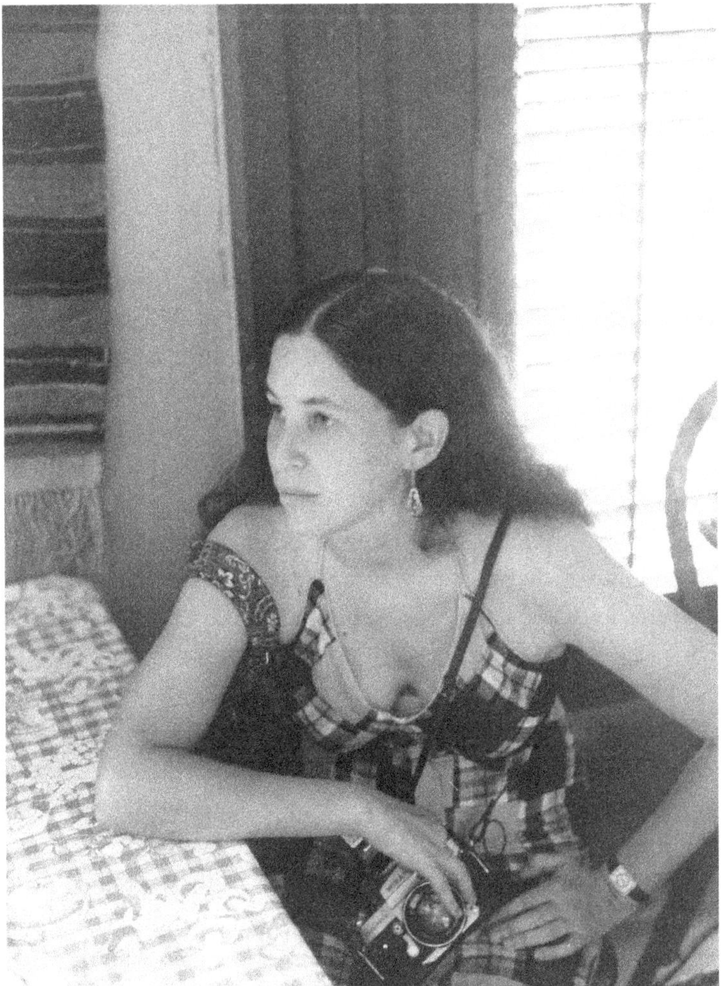

Mug Shots with Fellow Fugitives

The girl in a pink straw hat, which resembles a 1940s fedora, gazes into the California sky. In the photo, a cloud reflects off her pink sunglasses.

She stands on the grounds of the Hearst Castle in San Simeon. Is it the 1920s when it was built? The 1930s, the 1940s? She imagines all the movie stars, like Charlie Chaplin, who once visited.

This is her third trip.

Photos exist from each visit, but this one represents all of them—coalesced to a single image.

She believes in the mercurial timelessness of photographs. Whenever she looks at one, depending on mood or circumstance, a different truth is revealed; therefore, all are true at once whether the photo conjures love, joy, loss, rage, abandonment, nostalgia, emptiness. Each exposure atop another creates a palimpsest.

A man took the photograph. Once she knew him; now she doesn't. Like her first husband with whom she also visited the Hearst Castle, as well as her second. She knew them; now she doesn't.

People, movement suspended, mill around the background of the photos, other tourists. Their faces have become familiar to her. She feels as if she knows them, especially since the men who took the photographs of her are never in the frame. As if they're spying on her. Her psyche.

In the Visitors Center are photographs of famous actors who once vacationed at the Castle. Their faces, from old movies, are likewise impersonally familiar, whether she ever saw them in an actual movie or not.

She wonders if she, in her pink straw fedora, is captured in photos taken by other tourists. When they see her, what might they think? She looks at them, while they look at her.

Surely the familiarity of their faces is an illusion. A double exposure. Can the men who snapped the pictures identify her any better than those lurking in the background?

The answer is always no, if anyone would come forward to answer at all.

The Poetic Sentence

The skin on the prisoners' forearms appears tender. Over-exposed. Frail. Chaffing against starched orange jumpsuits. The men, about fifteen of them, sit at school desks in a room called the Library, though few books line the shelves. Here, in the State of Georgia, Floyd County Jail, they seem scared of me, afraid to make eye-contact, though I'm only armed with paper and pencils. And a poetry anthology.

The inmate population is always in flux. Therefore, every Tuesday evening when I arrive, I introduce myself, first name only, as instructed by the warden, a man who doesn't want me here in any event.

He believes poetry—he says the word with an emphasis on "po," without the "e"—is a waste of time on these "crimnals." *You got nothin' better to do than waste time teachin' potry to crimnals?*

Which leads me to consider why these men committed crimes that landed them in prison in the first place. Because no one taught poetry to them in this poor county? Because of emotional poverty? A poverty of love? The poverty of poverty?

When I first asked the warden's permission to teach, he accused me of being "a bleedin'-heart, do-gooder liberal." I nodded and let it go at that, though my decision to apply was spur of the moment. I'd been aimlessly driving around the countryside, along Calhoun Highway, when I spotted a trail of orange jumpsuits behind a razor-wire fence. I parked my car, entered the lobby, and asked to speak to the warden.

And while I *am* a bleeding-heart liberal, especially in this conservative county, my reasons to teach here are more complicated. I've seen these men on the *outside*. Not these particular men, of course, but close enough. I've been robbed at gunpoint on a late-night street in DC. I was threatened by a man and his knife in Boston. I was assaulted under a boardwalk at the Jersey shore. Those men were probably never caught, never locked away in prison. But maybe teaching these men in this jail will give me insight, understanding.

Besides, teaching a poetry class will help pad my thin resume.

"Right," I replied to the warden. "I *don't* have anything better to do." I smiled, waiting for him to not smile back.

I teach during a damp-gray winter, a magnolia spring, a humid-green summer, a rusty autumn, but seasons are obliterated by cinder block walls, sweat, and unrelenting fluorescent lights too scared to flicker. A plate-glass window covers one wall overlooking more cinder blocks painted the color of egg yolks. Most of the men attend class to see a woman. Any woman. Others, because it's slightly more entertaining than the desolation of their cells.

I begin the evening by reading a poem. I ask them to tell me what images they like, how the details make them feel. In truth, they don't like any of the poems. They shuffle feet in their white paper slippers as if they are scared of *me*. Scared that I am a woman who understands jagged lines of words? Scared because, in their macho world, poetry is, or should be, a jingle on television? Or a love song on a 3 a.m. country-western radio station?

Or are they scared because I don't seem scared of them?

After a halting discussion shot through with silence, it's time for them to write a poem attempting to replicate an image or feeling from the one I read.

As the men struggle to compose their confused feelings, they stare at the ceiling. Or they bend over their pieces of paper. Each grips a pencil as if never having held one before. Or never held one to write about *them, themselves* . . . who they are.

Or who they want to be.

Who they will or won't be after steel doors finally slide open. After they've served their sentences.

Regardless of whether I recite Emily Dickinson, Amiri Baraka, Ralph Ellison, Lucille Clifton, or Walt Whitman, their own poems are tattooed hearts pierced with arrows.

These men—convicted drug dealers, embezzlers, rapists, murderers—all miss girlfriends, mothers, children, wives.

As much as the men don't understand their actions on the outside, I'm not sure I understand mine here on the inside. I don't know the answer to the warden's question: *Nothin' better to do?* In addition to padding my resume, am I here because I feel satisfaction witnessing dangerous men locked up? Maybe, used as I am to violence, I deliberately seek it, or its origins? Is it curiosity? Who *are* these men who cause such mayhem on the outside? Do I want to see them here, where *I* hold the power, and they have none?

Or do they?

Sure, guards watch us, but what would happen if the inmates lunged at me? All I carry is a little pink briefcase containing ungraded essays and books for the community college where I teach part-time. I am always checked before steel doors slide open, then clang closed behind me.

I have no mace or pepper spray, no knife. But here, in this finely calibrated ecosystem—a balance between victim and predator—if one inmate makes a move toward me, roles switch. He would be doubly punished.

But that isn't what I want.

Do I actually think a few poems will make a difference?

The men are more interested in me than in poetry. Every Tuesday they ask questions about my husband (they've noticed my wedding band), whether I have children, where I work, where I live. Their voices, unlike when struggling with poetry, are animated and desperate, desperate to hold on to what I represent: the outside world.

The warden forbids me to respond to anything personal.

Still they ask.

And every week the men urge me to mail their poems to girlfriends, mothers, children, wives.

Just send it this once to my baby's mama.

They know I'm not allowed, but maybe they hope *this* time a reprieve will be granted. As if thin pleas with smudged words of love could fly out into the world.

"No," I say, my smile momentarily freezing. As if I'm saying, *Don't, get away from me, stop.* "You know I can't."

Maybe I come here seeking my own reprieve, a release from anger and fear that tattoos my own heart. A commutation of my own sentence.

Toward the end of the evening some of the men read what they've written. Their words, spoken aloud, do not exactly confess or ask forgiveness but come as close as they dare.

Missing the Clues

The male detective in the front row watches me, me in my lilac dress, as I deliver a presentation on child abuse prevention. I watch him, too, the safety of his presence, his gun, his gear. The audience gathered in this hotel meeting room consists of therapists, clinicians, law enforcement—people trained to save children—though no one, years ago, saved me, despite the evidence. The conference is taking place not far from the shore of Lake Michigan, close to where I live.

I've only swum in the lake once, this cold foreign water, so different from the Caribbean where I grew up. Different from the Gulf of Mexico, having lived in Galveston for eight years. Although fresh water is the color of shark skin, no predators shadow Lake Michigan, whereas saltwater swarms with stingrays, barracuda, jellyfish, sharks, and who-knows-what. Yet I plunged into the Caribbean's and Gulf's saltiness in confetti-colored bathing suits courting danger, though not, back then, concerned about threats.

After the presentation, the detective invites me for a drink at the hotel bar. He wears a gray-and-black uniform and a wedding ring. Despite all that, after a few beers, he invites me to his hotel room. What is he thinking? What have *I* been thinking? Surely now, after years of therapy, I know better. Now, I don't want to go to a hotel room with a detective. I want to *be* the detective. I want to be the bullet. I want to be the gun.

On Liminality

I was between husbands, living on a shoestring. By day I dazed through secretarial temp jobs at various oil companies averaging five dollars an hour. By night I worked at Disc Records in Almeda Mall earning four bucks an hour.

[ ]

After my day job I slogged through rush-hour heading north on the Gulf Freeway in my green un-air-conditioned vw beetle, inhaling exhaust, grit, diesel, and minor regret.

After the cold downtown office buildings, my body felt shocked by the swamp of late-afternoon Houston.

[ ]

I didn't turn on the car's *Blaupunkt* because the record store would be blasting its musical sales pitch all night long.

[ ]

The loudest sounds in the oil companies were the clacking of IBM Selectric typewriters and phones ringing in new gushers. But the bland corporate carpeting muted even that noise.

At the smaller companies, which only needed receptionist services, the phones barely rang. Otherwise bored, I read Proust's *Remembrance of Things Past*.

[ ]

Not that I wanted to remember my own past. Not that I even understood it. One day, it seemed, I was living with my husband, the next day, I wasn't. True, we'd each had affairs, but there were no fights, no recriminations.

I simply packed a white canvas Navy jacket, miniskirts, halter tops, and sandals, leaving behind gold-plated flatware, a marble table from Portugal, a hand-crafted couch, photographs, crystal candlesticks, woven rugs, sheets, pillows, all the wedding presents, and a husband.

[ ]

I moved into a furnished efficiency, a place containing other people's memories. Just as well. Let *those* memories float, undisturbed and hidden, on closet floors and under beds. Soon, I figured, my own memories would join them, operating here on the philosophy "out of sight out of mind." A good slogan for a moving company: *If you want to forget . . .*

[ ]

Not that I needed a moving company. All my belongings fit into my VW.

[ ]

Not that I needed a husband I never knew, would never know, either. I never learned how to penetrate his silent, immobile, immutable exterior to reach what, if anything, dwelled within.

Certainly as much my own failing as his.

[ ]

Now I traveled from the whispery silence of oil companies to the pulse of the record store, where customers asked where to find *this*, *this*, and *that*.

[ ]

At Almeda Mall I re-entered the arctic-conditioned chill of pretend-Houston.

I passed Foley's department store with its peacock-blue awnings and a plastic azalea replacing the apostrophe in the name.

[ ]

Disc Records was tucked between the Piccadilly Cafeteria and the Gold Mine Arcade. My feet felt the throb of bass before I heard Led Zeppelin, Steppenwolf, the Bee Gees, Donna Summer.

Records were alphabetically arranged by genre in giant bins: Classical, Rock 'n' Roll, Heavy Metal, Motown, R&B, Classic Rock, Reggae, Disco, Country-Western, Folk, Big Band, Gospel, Easy Listening.

No cross-over. Not possible to meld drums with zithers, say. It was a library: each category in its own space. No surprises. You wouldn't suddenly find the Village People in Easy Listening or Dvořák in Disco.

[ ]

The arrangement of albums was more dependable than the arrangement of people. Even myself. In which category would I put myself? "Adulterer"? "Divorcée"? "Existential Crisis"? "Loser"? I felt like Eleanor Rigby, as if all those lonely people sprang to life (or death or limbo) in Houston, Texas.

[ ]

Sometimes, at the oil companies, I was given an adding machine and long rows of numbers to add or subtract, multiply or divide. Scrolls of meaningless numbers. Was I calculating gallons of oil? The price of crude? The salaries of CEOs minus the wages of temp workers until they equaled greed?

Yet I felt a certain satisfaction when I finished, when each column was neat, accurate, precise.

Which made me hope I myself could (maybe) pass for neat, accurate, precise.

[ ]

On Liminality 93

At the end of the evening, albums were strewn everywhere. Before we could clock out, all had to be re-binned so the morning crew would find a well-ordered store: neat, accurate, precise.

[ ]

My marriage had been so well-ordered we could ignore each other altogether. He lived in one bin, I another. Rarely did our off-key or divergent hearts cross over into the other's bin.

[ ]

Sometimes browsing customers slid records into the wrong category, so every week we flipped through every bin to see whether, for example, Beethoven found himself beside Loretta Lynn, a bad match, or Queen beside Perry Como, a worse match.

(David Bowie and Bing Crosby *did* record a Christmas song together, which was a hit, but that was only a single.)

[ ]

Periodically, out of low-grade despair, I deliberately mis-shelved albums, slipping, say, an Easy Listening album (*25 Romantic Songs to Fall in Love*) beside Steppenwolf's self-titled debut featuring their successful single "Born to Be Wild."

I threw in Frank Sinatra's *Strangers in the Night* for good measure.

[ ]

I didn't know if I was looking for romance or if I was born to be wild. Or neither.

Or both.

Definitely, I was a stranger to myself every night.

[ ]

At the record store I was given a half hour off for dinner, unpaid. To save money, I brought a peanut butter and jelly sandwich and a banana from home. I found a bench in the Pineapple Fountain Court after begging a glass of water from Piccadilly's. Here, the background music was an indistinguishable din of voices, footsteps, the rustle of shopping bags, the tinkling of the fountain. And Muzak.

Children tossed coins into the water. Periodically a child tumbled in, causing parents to shriek.

I heard no one and everyone. Nothing and everything. I was surrounded by people all day: at the oil companies, at the mall. At night, in my apartment complex, I felt besieged by neighbors. For brief moments, I focused on individuals, even talked when necessary. But no conversation—or even a passing glance—lingered. I blazed past each encounter leaving behind only a sliver of burnt city grit.

[ ]

At a nearby bench in the Pineapple Fountain Court an elderly couple silently ate a French Poodle Supreme—hot dogs and French fries—from Le Petit.

I pretended *I* was part of an elderly couple who had survived the decades. Who had an uninterrupted history with memories.

[ ]

Except I had an interrupted history with porous vectors, memories floating through me or, at times, lingering long enough to remind me I had no one with whom to eat a French Poodle Supreme.

[ ]

It never occurred to me to seek a better job. Before I married and moved to Texas, I worked on Capitol Hill in DC. Those skills didn't seem to translate to Texas. Or I couldn't understand the drawl, or myself, to figure out how to find a bin where I belonged.

[ ]

Years later, with a second husband, living in a different state, I applied to a program to get a master's degree in social work. Miraculously, given my spectacular lack of qualifications, I was accepted. But still not knowing my own bin—I'd merely substituted one lost-cause marriage for another—I was only smart enough to know I couldn't help anyone else find their bin, either.

I tossed the acceptance letter.

[ ]

At night, back in my efficiency, I listened to my neighbors through thin walls. Truthfully, I was disappointed by the lack of drama: no shouting, no throwing of pots and pans, no crying children. It was as if the heavy Houston air, scented with crude floating up from refineries in Texas City, flattened everyone's spirit in this end-of-the-road apartment complex.

[ ]

Other nights, unable to sleep, I drove Houston's interstates and freeways, around the loop, past the Astrodome and Astroworld, Meyerland Plaza, Finger's Furniture, Wyatt's Cafeteria, Hobby Airport, Shepherd's Drive-in, past exits for the Katy Freeway, Almeda-Genoa, Buffalo Bayou, League City, the NASA Space Center, heading south toward the Causeway and Galveston Island, where my ex-husband still lived.

I followed taillights, blasted past headlights, driving inside the outside lines—or was it outside the inside lines—but stuck in a liminal space.

[ ]

Sometimes I thought about living in the Almeda Mall, which sold everything to eat, drink, wear, want. Banks, travel agents, guns and ammo, stationery, pipes, hairdressers and barbers, candy, movies, tickets to concerts, ice cream, books, nuts, drapery cleaning.

Everything *for* a life but not a life itself.

[ ]

Foley's plastic Aztec sun decoration resplendently shone down on all.

[ ]

One of the oil companies offered me a permanent job for $6.50 an hour. But permanent is permanent. I turned it down.

[ ]

At Christmas, the oil companies were not as busy, had less need for temp help, while the record store asked if I could work longer hours.

Fake trees were decorated with angel figurines, tinsel, and lights. Christmas carols usurped Aerosmith. The manager asked employees to wear cheery red. I clipped on a red plastic carnation to adorn my hair.

[ ]

Santa Claus arrived by helicopter, landing in the giant parking lot outside Foley's.

[ ]

I still ate lunch by the Pineapple Fountain, watching couples and families weighted with fancy wrapped packages. I refused to think of their houses scented with apple pies and cinnamon candles.

I bought no presents and received none.

[ ]

No Christmas bonus. Not even a ham.

[ ]

On Christmas Eve, after I closed the store, I paused in the deserted corridor. Displays, now unlit, shadowed the panes of glass. Green and silver garlands still swayed in processed air.

At Easter, plastic bunnies would be displayed.
At Halloween . . .
For Valentine's Day . . .
For the Fourth of July . . .
Everything looked the same; everything appeared different.

[ ]

These corridors themselves were liminal spaces, like my marriage, or my life, where no connections—no exits/entrances—existed.

I wasn't moving forward or backward.

Each minute repeated itself.

It was like hallways of hospitals or airports or cheap motels at three o'clock in the morning.

All I heard was static.

Exchange Rates

1.

I step off the DC Transit bus after work, returning home to my apartment, when a man rushes up to me, breathless. He wears a suit and tie, hair neatly combed, not like the hippies draped around the fountain in DuPont Circle. He carries a briefcase. He's already smiling as he blocks my path on the sidewalk gasping, "Hello."

He speaks quickly. I only catch random words: *Lost wallet. Home. Wife. Kids. Ten dollars.* My eyebrows rise at the amount. Sensing I'm about to step away, his story continues about needing a taxi. Medicine? Groceries? I'm listening and not.

From his tumble of words, I'm almost in a trance. His words slur my mind. Why, of all the people around, does he approach me in my love beads and miniskirt?

He needs me. I can help him. Save the day. Save him?

I shrug my embroidered hippie satchel off my shoulder. Open my wallet. Give him two fives.

A week later, in the *Washington Post*, I read an article about a con man who approaches women at bus stops.

2.

After I leave home for college—years after my father no longer, overtly, misloves me—he still gives me money. Even after I have a job. Even after I marry. When I visit, he hugs me, pressing twenty-dollar bills into my hand. His scent of Old Spice is like a flashback; I'm a little girl again.

Other times, he wants to give me more. Five hundred dollars. A thousand. He'll write me a check, he says. He has an account separate from the one he shares with his wife, my mother. He says she'll never find out. *Our secret*, he whispers.

Growing up, he always taught me to say "yes." To never say "no." At least not to him. To men like him.

I want my father's money. I don't want it. I want something, something that has nothing to do with money.

3.

In my thirties, when I live in Georgia with my second husband, I enter therapy in a clinic housing about ten practitioners. One of them, not my own therapist, always seems to hover in the lobby when I arrive, the same time each week. He has a black braid, wears denims and a t-shirt, one turquoise earring. I learn he's not an officially degreed therapist but helps clients heal through use of essential oils, herbs, and meditation.

One particular day, after my therapy session, I pass his office, the door ajar. He calls to me to enter . . . enter this space scented with eucalyptus and sage, a meditation tape playing in the background. He invites me to sit on the couch. As we talk, whisper, really, he leaves the door open only a crack, as if I'm a secret, so my therapist won't see us if he walks down the hall.

Am I here to be in the presence of meditation, eucalyptus, sage, or the man who teaches the properties of them?

Week after week I enter his office, not as a client. Now, he sits beside me on the couch. He holds my hand. He hugs me. He tells me about having fought three tours of duty in Vietnam. He explains he initially discovered this healing profession for himself, as he suffers from PTSD.

One week he confides that his young child is sick; he doesn't have money to pay for treatment. He asks if I can loan him a thousand dollars, promising to pay it back in a month.

I write out a check.

4.

A thousand dollars, just like that, is debited from my checking account. It's money I saved from my part-time teaching job at a community college, earmarked for therapy sessions.

Or a thousand dollars that could purchase more than ten pairs of shoes. New dresses. New brakes for my Volkswagen bug that I bought secondhand for under a thousand dollars. How many books? A vacation. New furniture. Rent.

Or do I think this man with the black braid will love me if I loan him a thousand dollars? How much do I need his love?

Will the thousand dollars save his sick child? Is his child sick? Does he have a child?

Did my father think I'd forgive him if he gave me *money, money, money*?

How much is money actually worth? What can it buy?

What is love worth?

Or a soul?

After I give the man with the black braid the check, one month passes. Two. Three.

Now, when I come to the clinic for therapy, his office door is closed. He no longer invites me to sit on his couch.

Finally, I tell my therapist what happened.

The next week, my therapist hands me a check for a thousand dollars, given to him from the man with the black braid.

As I leave the clinic with the check, the door to the black-braid man's office is wide open. The couch is gone. The meditation tape is silent. No scent of eucalyptus. Maybe a residue of burning sage.

I miss him. I don't miss him. I miss something. Something I would pay better money for, but better money doesn't exist.

Remembrance of Things Past

I walked home from high school in Glen Rock, New Jersey, in a wintry dusk. I clasped my books and homework, zippered in a leatherette case, to my chest, another layer of insulation. I wore a suede jacket trimmed with fake white fur. Yet soft. Comforting around my neck. My loafers tapped still-snowless suburban sidewalks. My knees were frigid above my socks. But with this solitary shock of cold, the rest of me warmed. The scent of fireplace smoke deepened the air.

I whispered lines to a poem I had to memorize, a school assignment.

Now, all these years later, I can't recall the poem or even the title.

Yet I remember timing my footfalls to match the syllables of the lines.

I remember, at some point along the two-mile walk, singing, although just in my head, the song "Crying" by Roy Orbison.

Despite the lyrics, I felt alone more than sad, a sense of solitude more than unhappiness.

I didn't feel like crying.

I don't feel like crying.

Venus hovered in the purple sky. Nightfall was a path to follow across the universe as stars switched on one by one, like lamps inside the homes I passed.

I suppose I successfully memorized the assigned poem, only to forget it. Maybe it will come back to me one day, the way sensations of that moment return to me now.

How content I feel, my senses fully alive with that evening—small, yet also vast—like a poem.

The Long Road Out of Eden

One late afternoon after work, as a college intern on Capitol Hill, I sit on a sunny porch in a house off Wisconsin Avenue with an older woman, a friend of my parents. A spotless white cloth covers a patio table. Yellow dishes match the pitcher of lemonade. Silverware gleams. I'm too young to know the diplomatic language of adults, so I'm unable to tell the woman about the worm in the beautiful strawberry plucked from her own garden. I'm holding the strawberry in my fingers, about to take a bite.

Must I eat the strawberry? Is there a delicate way to tug the worm from the red, seeded flesh without the woman noticing?

I'm fraught with indecision, especially since the woman, single and in her forties, seems to live with no indecisions whatsoever. She never wanted to marry, she told me. She bought this house on her own. She's an assistant to the secretary of the Department of Agriculture.

"First job out of college," she says. "I started at Agriculture as a receptionist. I worked my way up the ladder."

The woman had invited me to dinner to help guide me on the ins-and-outs of a career in government.

The woman's cotton blouse and skirt are starched and fresh. Her hair appears sculpted with hairspray, her fingernails coral. After taking a DC Transit bus from Capitol Hill, I feel wrinkled, my hair a wild, ambiguous frizz.

In addition to my indecision about the worm, I'm uncertain about my future (unlike the woman). I'll graduate from college in one year. Should I return to Capitol Hill and work my way up the career ladder? Buy a house? Marry? Children? Should I plant my own garden but beware of worms in strawberries?

I consider how the woman, who works for the Department of Agriculture, should know about pesticides. But pesticides are poison. And the worm, were it not in the strawberry, just inches from my lips, would be innocently worming between blades of grass.

Back then, did I eat the strawberry? I don't remember. Nor do I recall if I ate the worm, or if I told the woman about it.

Yet I long for that moment of possibilities, my future undecided. Sitting on that porch, listening to the woman, I couldn't foresee how I would marry, would, in fact, have too many ex-husbands, how I would never work my way up a career ladder, never have children, or plant a garden.

What I remember, now no longer a girl, is the sun-warmth on my young, bare shoulders on a late-afternoon porch. And what I will miss is that one almost-perfect strawberry. Or was it perfect, anyway, even with the worm?

POSTCARD   *Greetings from Atlantic City!*   PLACE STAMP HERE

Dear Future Me,

I want *to want* to fly like the wind—the way Dad rides his bike up and down the boardwalk, the way Sis jogs for hours.

But, like Mom, I kind of hate *movement*. I try to avoid sightseeing because I love the stillness of non-movement. When I tramp around looking at *this*, experiencing *that*, it's like I can't hold onto my thoughts. They scatter in the wind. Distracted.

So Mom and I sit on a bench on the boardwalk overlooking the Atlantic. I unwrap pieces of saltwater taffy, sucking them one by one. Oh, and that hazy sun, seemingly suspended, a round absence in the sky.

Love,
Sue

The Undertaking

You and your stoned boyfriend, Paul, sit on the floor of his sparse college apartment on Commonwealth Avenue in Boston listening to "Light My Fire." By the hour. Well, you listen to the entire Doors album, but particularly that song. Paul, his face pale and thin, like he hasn't eaten in a week, sits on one side of the stereo, on a mothy Oriental rug, you on the other. His eyes are closed, his head against the wall. You only know he hasn't completely passed out because his foot moves in time to the beat. Or slightly off-beat. Marijuana scares you. You are not stoned, yet feel it, or feel something, in the late afternoon scented with weed, sandalwood incense, patchouli, and a kind of indefinable hippie fume of tie-dye scarves, fake-bronze Buddhas, plastic love beads, and inertia.

Paul wants to have sex with you, which is to say intercourse. To delay the "event," you've told him you're a virgin. This is a complete untruth. Or, as the song lyrics suggest: *I would be a liar.* Now, deep into the lie, you don't know how to backtrack. Nor are you sure you want to. You don't know how to explain about the drugs, that you don't know who the *real* Paul is. How would he even interpret your fear in his hazy smoky daze?

What would sex be like with a man you may or may not love or even fully know? He claims to love you. But is stoned love *real*?

Well, of course you *have* had sex with men you didn't love, but at least they were breathing. And conscious. Which sometimes you worry Paul isn't. Not too much to ask.

The Doors took their name from Aldous Huxley's book *The Doors of Perception*, about how drugs expand consciousness. But doesn't expansion first require consciousness?

Much of the 1960s is about achieving love and enlightenment, but in a biography about Jim Morrison, Stephen Davis asserts that the Doors' music is about "endarkenment."

On the album cover, Morrison, like Paul, has dark curly hair as well as an emaciated distance in the eyes that resembles rambling miles of desert trails full of strange nothingness.

Even so, Morrison's face exerts a smoldering sexuality, which you love. He is a dangerous man (most assuredly) but safe because he is unreachable, transcendent, if regressively so. Paul, on the other hand, is a safe man (probably, mostly) but dangerous because he is close-by real.

Later that evening, Paul lies in bed. You sit beside him, not sure if he's awake. His skin is so pallid you decide, on the spur of the moment, to apply your makeup to his face. You dab pale green on his lids, a color that matches your hazel eyes rather than his gray ones. You accentuate them with black liner, curling the lashes black as well. You dust iridescent blush across his cheeks, a shimmering gloss on his lips. Paul's only movement, as you lean close to him, is a slight and silent rise and fall to his chest.

The night is quiet. No voices from neighbors. No traffic racing down Commonwealth. A haze of weed and incense drifts in from the living room. You step back from him. Even in candlelight, he appears frosty—cool rather than warm. You shiver. With makeup, he looks gaudy as a dead rock star.

You can't imagine your head resting on the pillow beside him.

You whisper out the flame. You leave the room, closing the door behind you.

In the not-too-distant future, Jim Morrison will die in a bathtub in Paris, that city of romance and light. Death is the opposite of living, darkness the opposite of light, but what is the opposite of romance? Is there one?

After Morrison's death, his gravesite in Père Lachaise Cemetery becomes the site of a pilgrimage for his fans, who love him madly. So madly that the gravesite is marred by graffiti, frequently vandalized. It's as if Morrison and his fans (including you) embrace a fulminating romance, which death both does and does not stop.

Reflections on *Blue Velvet*

Four of you, two women, two men, married but not to each other, sneak away from a conference to see the movie. It's about good and evil. Innocence and experience. The commonplace versus mystery. After the movie, late now, none of you want to return to the conference and re-enter the world of everyday conversation with the other attendees.

You drive into the dark Vermont countryside and park by a lake. You all decide to take off your clothes and swim.

Is it to cleanse the movie from your skin or to plunge deeper into its corruption?

The water barely laps the sandy, rocky shore. A wedge of moon rippling the lake is the only light. You wonder what the darkness of the surrounding forest is hiding, or whether the rhythm of the movie underscores the moment to make it something it's not. *Is* this an ordinary night in Vermont or are the four of you becoming extraordinary, like the characters in the movie, even though you aren't?

You hold the hand of one of the men as you cross the shore. Having removed his glasses, he stumbles, apologizes, claiming an astigmatism in one eye. You, too, have an astigmatism but don't wear glasses, preferring a slightly hazy, blurry world.

Almost under water, you want to kiss the man but don't.

You want to be simultaneously enveloped by good and evil, innocence and experience, the commonplace and the mysterious. But you don't know how to achieve it.

It's a strange world, the protagonist in the movie says.

All you have are the coolness of water on your body and the warmth of the man's hand in yours.

Later you return to the conference, your own separate rooms. The next day it's as if the evening before never happened.

None of you mention the movie, the lake, the knowledge that you'll never experience shadowy blue mysteries of other worlds, only the mystery of this one, without a director to tell you what to do next.

The Family *Chiroptera*

1.

My future second ex-husband and I sit around Rick and Beth's kitchen table in damp swimsuits, the first time the four of us dine together. Rick pours drinks while Beth arranges cheese and crackers. Outside the sliders, their two children, a boy and girl, splash in the pool. We spent the afternoon swimming, sunning on lounges, before coming inside. Rick, a paleontologist at a local college in Georgia, explains his research project at a bat cave north of town, how we learn more about the origin of life through bats and mice than dinosaurs.

I, myself, want to learn more about why, almost imperceptibly, Rick's knee grazes mine under the table.

Beth, I'm sure, notices.

"You should show Sue the cave," Beth says. Her smile, however, is tight.

I teach night classes and, childless, am free all day. Beth and my soon-to-be ex-husband have full-time jobs, he at the same college as Rick.

What I'll remember years later: The everyday details of family life. The laughter of children, the scent of pine straw and chlorine, steaks on the grill, the radio turned to an oldies station, the slow swirl of the overhead fan, the first hint of evening softening light . . . that almost childhood longing, belief, that summer lasts forever. I want the dinner to last for weeks.

Months.

Rick grazes my knee again. The spell is broken.

2.

Rick and I alight from his Jeep Cherokee after driving increasingly rutted red clay roads into the forests of North Georgia, the foothills of the Appalachians. We walk along a path of matted grass. Rick points out ash, sugarberry, beech, and buckeye trees. He knows the names of *things*, whereas to me things are merely trees, birds, insects, interchangeable—like lovers.

Last night, when Beth suggested I accompany Rick, I shrugged and tried to decline. But not hard enough. It's as if her words set off a chain-reaction preventing free will, though of course that's a lie. I *could* have declined. I didn't.

What I'll regret years later: How, at the time, Rick's eyes seemed soft as the two long syllables of "azure." That I couldn't see them as merely blue.

3.

In a sack, Rick carries a flashlight, a flask of water, graph paper, and pencils. We reach the cave entrance and stare into a starless, underground sky. Am I more interested in the origin of life than terrified of bats and mice? A bat once tangled in my long hair when I was a girl living in St. Thomas. I, well, *batted* at it, screaming. It flew away.

"The bats are Eastern Pipistrelle, or tri-colored bats," he says.

I wonder if they're color coordinated, which makes me think I'd just as soon be with Beth, bargain shopping for outfits at Marshall's. Why did she urge me to be with her husband? Has he done this before, and *she* knows this is inevitable?

What I don't think in the moment: I don't want Rick, or intrigue. Instead, I want Rick and Beth, their children, their life together. I want to be a member of their family, a *family, in a wishful, magical thinking way, not some crazy-stalker-woman-movie way.*

I think.

4.

The air cools immediately when we enter the cave. Rick shines the flashlight, illuminating mounds of guano. I step around it and its musty scent of ammonia.

Rick's voice echoes as he explains about 1,200 species of bats, 14 of which live in North Georgia. They belong to the family *Chiroptera*, which means "hand wing." They are the only flying mammal.

He kneels beside a mound of guano, although he's also looking for mouse droppings. At his request, I hold the flashlight while he draws lines on graph paper, a matrix tracking the movement of mice he discerns through their droppings.

I try to avoid thinking about bats, mice, and why I'm here with Rick.

Last night, the four of us, six with their children, ate bowls of ice cream after dinner. We stood by the sliders watching water softly undulate in the lit pool. Neighborhood lights sprinkled across the hills, the moon rising. Rick stood beside me. We weren't touching, yet I felt him, the way you feel summer heat rising off concrete.

I was already singed, even as I longed for the perfection of a life where a family stands by open sliders eating ice cream, enveloped by the cool fullness of evening, not the absence of sunlight.

I'll long for this moment years later but more as hiraeth, a homesickness for a past that never quite was . . . or could never have been.

5.

Outside the cave again, we drink from the flask of water. Civilization seems distant. No cars or voices. Only insects whirring in long grasses, leaves rustling. Rick sets down his sack of supplies. Even his smile resembles something you might see at the end of civilization: cool, dark, as if we'd spent hours in the cave.

Weeks.

Months.

Millennia.

Rick kisses me. A droplet of water from his mustache, which tastes as if it arose from an abandoned underground well, dampens my upper lip.

What I'll only envision years later is the hard light of the sky after the darkness of the cave—that color brittle enough to crack.

My future ex-husband and I will be invited to attend more family dinners.

Until we're not.

The Soft Beauty of an Ordinary Life

Before his wife catches you:

One spring evening in Georgia, you slide onto the passenger seat of Rick's Jeep Cherokee outside a Big Lots. You secretly meet here, Thursdays, in this anonymous location, to head north into the foothills of the Appalachians. At dusk, the lights of this box store appear like an oasis across the vast cement stretch of parking lot, across the endless boredom of the week, since the last time you were together.

After his wife catches you:

You imagine walking tracks of a railroad through a forest. Under your feet you hear gravel crunching like bones. Wind tangles branches of trees, and bark creaks in an otherwise silent day. You don't know if this railroad line leads away from your unforgivable past or toward what will be an unforgiveable future. Or both.

Before his wife catches you:

You and he lie on a blanket of moist grass beside too-sweet fumes of magnolias. Night insects agitate the air with more passion than your own, which wears a deceitful mask of love. Over his shoulder a sickle moon slices the sky; if only it'd slice you in two, then you wouldn't remember the number of men preceding this one. You wouldn't remember the history of your emotional misdemeanors.

Because this isn't your first affair.

You already know your proclamation of love is false. As is his. Except in every amnesiac fantasy, you temporarily forget.

You're terrified that sex, this mysterious yet ordinary act, might be all you've known. You wear it like a plaster cast holding body parts together. Or you embrace it as an antidote to loneliness, melancholy, loss, boredom, despair. So how can this desire be temporary?

After his wife catches you:
Your heart *thrums* as you walk the railroad tracks, but your chest feels empty, as if air is unbreathable. The destruction you've caused is a scar carved through a forest.

Before his wife catches you:
You vaguely notice headlights sweep across your nude bodies.

When his wife catches you:
A slash of blonde hair. Words like shards of stars rip the sky, piercing your eyes. *Slut*, to you. *Bastard*, to him. You close your lids, now gritty with disgrace.

After his wife catches you:
The scent of magnolia is a memento of remembrance. You want the white petals to drug you into forgetfulness.

After you and he are caught:
His wife slams back into her Honda. She guns the engine, spewing leaves and pine straw across your naked bodies. Stinging you with dirt. Muddying your skin. You and he silently dress, your clothes damp from evening forest dew. You don't look at each other as you walk toward his car. You quietly close the door as if you're a whisper lost to the sound of mist. Pine trees sway as if their tops bow in shame. He puts his Jeep in gear and pulls back onto the road.

Watching headlights of oncoming cars, you believe you see a mirage. Can you unlearn what you know? Can you not know what you see? That you will always hear her words behind the lids of your eyes.

He drives in silence, following the blacktop as if aiming toward the end of the earth.

Melodramatically, metaphorically, existentially, metaphysically, realistically, you *want* to plunge off the end of the earth. You want to open the car door and jump.

The double yellow lines on the asphalt are a warning: do not cross.

At Big Lots, he stops beside your car. Still not a word. Still can't look at him. This non-looking is the last time you don't see him.

What remains after you catch yourself:
You sit in your Ford Escort watching cars pull in and out of the parking lot. No one would find you here among shoppers carrying plastic bags containing towels, shoes, coffee mugs, laundry detergent, toothpaste, t-shirts, baby food, shampoo. Tangible things that compose a home, a family, the soft beauty of an ordinary life, one you don't yet know how to live.

Miss Demeanor Considers the Time She Stood under the Boardwalk at the Jersey Shore, a Location So Distant from Love That the Pillar Was All That Held Her Up in the Face of the Oncoming Storm

Jacket, black leather.
Girl, waiting for trouble.
Smile, knowing.

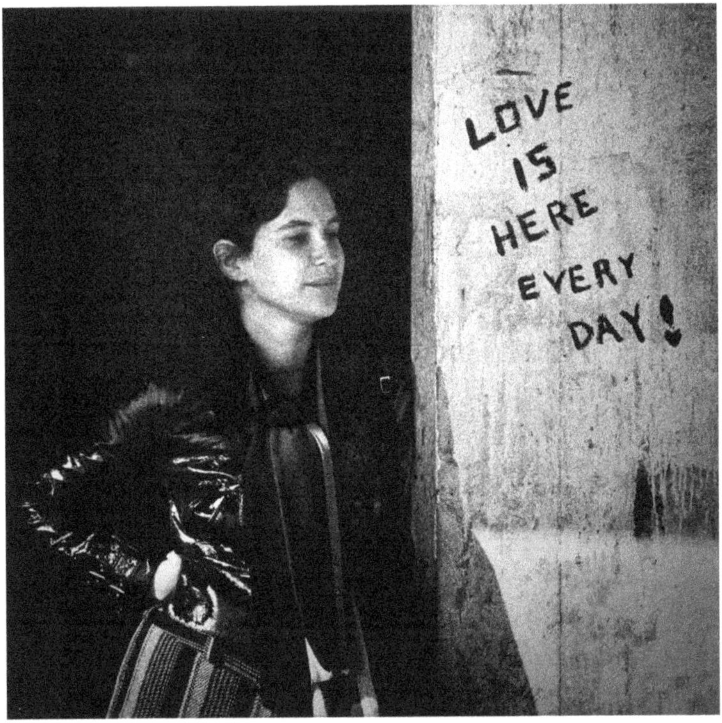
LOVE
IS
HERE
EVERY
DAY!

Trashy

Housecleaning takes time and effort.
—Consumer Reports Books, *How to Clean Practically Anything*

In bare feet, my soles slightly sticking to the dirty hardwood floor, I walk into the kitchen and eye the steel garbage can. With dread. Tomorrow is pick-up day. In twelve years, I've never taken out the trash. It was my husband's responsibility. But he left me two days ago, no advance warning, on the Fourth of July. Now, I hesitate before the can, seemingly unable, me a grown woman, to pull out the plastic bag.

My restored Victorian house, here in Michigan, sounds deserted. No male feet plod down creaky stairs. Distant shouts from kids filter through the screens. Neighbors, still celebrating Independence Day, laugh in their backyards. *Everyone will know my husband left me if they see me hauling out the trash.* But how long can I wait? A month? A year? Can I simply pile the bags in the kitchen until I die and let whoever finds me cart them off along with my carcass?

I flip open the lid. Fruit flies swarm into the air. With forefingers and thumbs, I tug the edge of the bag. More strength is required. I grip it tighter and yank. Once. Twice. The bag levitates from its container. I plop it on the floor.

Apple cores, scraps of meat, wadded napkins. Refuse from my husband: a banana peel, the pit from an avocado. The tuna can belongs to me. I'd forgotten to wrap the sharp top in a paper towel; a slit pierces plastic. Chicken bones from our last dinner together.

If our garbage disposal worked, there wouldn't be as much in the bag. But it broke our first day in the house, after we moved here from Georgia a year ago for my second husband's new job. Probably that was as clear a sign as any if I paid attention. Which, clearly, I did not. We never bothered to fix it. Never bothered to fix anything. Another sign? What does it say about a marriage when the husband and wife can't even adequately discard refuse?

The bag is white, the ties red. I knot them. Then knot them again as if the garbage is a secret. I don't want anyone to see inside.
I don't want anyone to see the garbage my husband left behind. Me, behind.

I lift the bag and head outside to the garage, to the rubberized receptacle. I pry off the top and drop the bag inside. Now, I must only wheel it to the end of the driveway, past a row of arbor vitae, under canopied branches of the maple arching over the drive. The plastic wheels clatter the pavement. I focus on this, no longer hearing shouts of children. Not seeing birds, tucking wings, preparing for evening. Not smelling the scent of family cookouts. Just me, the clatter, and my fingers gripping the handle.

Years ago, after graduating college, I lived alone in a high-rise efficiency apartment in Washington DC. Evenings, after work, I fixed myself a simple dinner. Every Saturday I vacuumed and dusted. I wiped kitchen counters. Cosmetics, toothbrush, toothpaste, comb—each had its proper place in the bathroom. Before sleep, I stood on the small balcony overlooking the city: the white pristine monuments, in spring the scent of cherry blossoms. Then I curled up on my sofa bed to read. Not that I owned the apartment, but it *felt* like mine. My job, my money, my schedule. Nothing to cause disruption. If I heard the next-door neighbors, well, they had nothing to do with me.
My garbage.
In that high-rise, I neatly placed it in a paper bag and slid it down the incinerator chute. Whenever I wanted. As if life itself could be spic-and-span. No residue. No messy marital discord. Even my emotions felt clean.

Miss Demeanor Considers the Time between Hippiedom and Adulthood When She Gazed into the Future as If to Swim to a Distant Shore, Yet Unable to Move Forward or Back

Cap, red.
Jacket, blue.
Girl, sad.

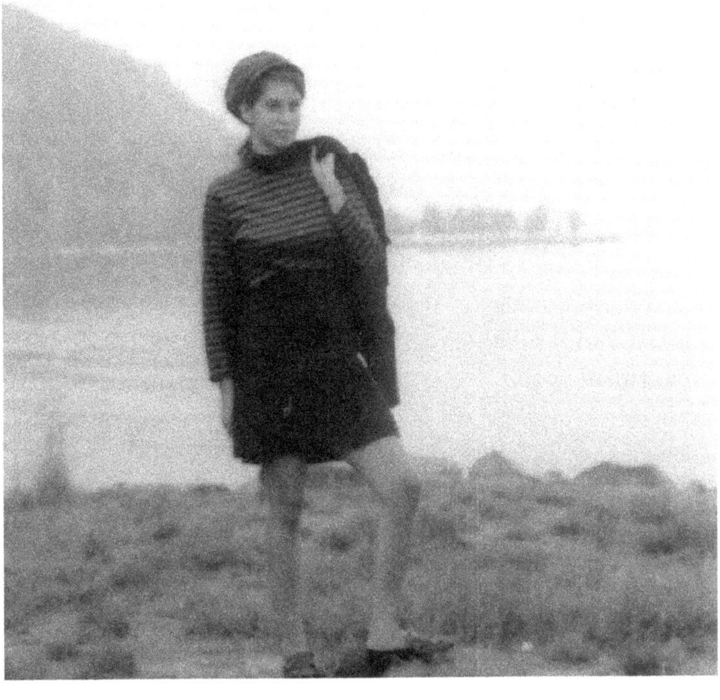

Degas Paints the Chippendales and Me

> The ballerinas in Degas' paintings appear artfully pristine. Look closer. In the 1800s, ballerinas were forced into sexual relationships with wealthy male patrons. The "foyer de la danse" where the dancers warmed up doubled as a men's club where patrons socialized and propositioned the ballerinas. Degas' works often feature shadowy figures lurking in the wings that contrast with the glittering figures on stage.
>
> —impressionistarts.com

Painting #1

A print of Degas's *L'Etoile*, the star ballerina wearing pink, hangs over my teenage bed, my room painted blue, ballet slippers on a blue oval rug. Before sleep, I reach down and slide the ribbony laces between my fingers. The scent of resin. The toe points are scuffed from skimming across wood floors. In this pastel impressionistic moment, this young girl dreams she's exceptional enough to be a prima ballerina at the Paris Opera. A star.

My father's nightly footsteps, interrupting dreams, shadow down the hall.

The fantasy quickens. Now, I must *glissade, sautér, elancer* far away from this bed, this room, this moment, to dance into a more elegant future.

Painting #2

As a freshman in college—no longer a ballerina but still my father's daughter—I fall in love with Forrest, the man old enough to be my father. When his wife is away, I glide across the street to his Back Bay apartment. He plays Frank Sinatra on the stereo, snow outside his window, flakes twirling past streetlamps against a twilight sky. Forrest wants me to embrace the music's sense of *dépaysé*—a sense of longing, he explains—but not necessarily longing or desire for a particular person or place. More a homesickness, a yearning, a feeling you almost capture but can't quite, even as it sways you.

When he embraces me on those winter nights, when we slow dance to "It Was a Very Good Year," I fear how easily his arms might release me. Will he, or I, merely drift into chiaroscuro: light into shade, shade into light? Will one day he, or I, be homesick for this one fleeting moment? If art can transform shadow into chiaroscuro, can we transform homesickness into love, even though we are not artists? Even though my father is the choreographer of my every step?

Painting #3

After college I aimlessly drift, seeking a "me." Evenings, I haunt stripper bars. I watch women in G-strings and tassels swirl around poles, careless legs spread toward drunk, urgent men. In the dim light, their bodies, a verdigris sheen, perform with the fatalistic, perhaps fantastical belief this is as good as it gets.

I sit alone in a bar sipping bored scotch. I glance at myself in the row of mirrors tiling the walls. In the cracks and smudges I—all of us—appear dismembered. Have the women, aged seventeen or thirty-seven, tumbled from the frame of a Degas after their final bow? The male patrons, shaded and murky, don't glance at me fully clothed. They focus on the gallery of dancers showcased in spotlights.

The strippers and I are almost pointillist, disconnected dots seeking to give the impression of being whole women. Not that anyone would notice, or could see, that connection.

Painting #4

In my thirties, in a Texas bar, wearing a low-cut blouse, short skirt, and spike heels, I watch Chippendale dancers. Unemployed and in a second loveless marriage, I want to feel the risk, the possibility, the rush of a night sexualizing nearly naked men, what men feel when they sexualize me. The dancers wear collared bowties and wrist cuffs mimicking Playboy Playmates. Their oiled chests ripple with muscles, bare skin descending to black spandex. Beads of sweat glisten as they strut across the stage.

Velcro-ed pants rip off the Chippendales' legs. The women in the audience, who wear too much perfume and too few inhibitions, stuff bills inside the men's G-strings. I, too, brought money but don't offer any. The Chippendales display too much of themselves, yet nothing at all.

How would Degas paint the Chippendales? Would he add tutus and tights? Would he cloak faces in veiled light, disguising how they feel?

Some Chippendales die of drug overdoses. Others surely feel diminished: a smudge of paint beneath a thumb.

How would Degas paint *me*? Would I be another featureless face in the darkness, at the edge of the canvas, peering? Devouring?

Painting #5

Not long after I watch the Chippendale performance, I attend a Halloween party dressed like a Playboy bunny. The costume, of course, is makeshift: a maroon bathing suit, a leather dog collar, black fishnet stockings, silver spike sandals. I glue on a cotton-ball tail.

How would Degas paint me here, now? How many shadow-men leer at me from the wings? I mean "shadow" as a verb: *hunt, track, trail, pursue*. I mean "me" as in a figure who should be repainted. Repented.

Painting #6

Dépaysé: actually, less a sense of longing than of displacement.

Pentimento: something painted over, which re-emerges. For example, could the joy of dancing be restored if you scraped away the overlay of grief?

Pink ballet slippers: frayed now, from pirouetting on shadows.

Part 3

Grieflets

> We couldn't stop drinking or talking or kissing the wrong people no matter what it ruined.
> —Paula McLain, *The Paris Wife*

Too

> He was mad, bad, and dangerous to know.
>
> —Lady Caroline Lamb (about Lord Byron)

I bite into a pear when the man responds, "I love you, too." *Too?* I swallow, holding the pear, not setting it on the ceramic plate. Fragile flowers swoon over the lip of a crystal vase. Silverware sparkles. Remains of a perfect dinner omelet, crumbs from a buttered baguette, scatter on dishes. Still, I hold the pear. I turn it. I take another bite. The word "too," which follows "you," replays, replays.

The night yard is blank behind plate-glass. His eyes—not blank—are too full of tomorrow's lies.

A furnace vibrates the tiled floor. Heat needles my skin. A shadow, disconnected from his absent wife, shades the cool-warm air. Like breath. But not.

I take another bite of pear. Sweetness, crunch, numb my tongue. When I finish, he will beckon me to another room. *That* room. Where he'll show me another lie, too.

Grieflets

Dressed in cut-off jeans and a stained tank top, I sit on my bedroom floor by the open window of my Georgia log cabin. I cradle the phone between shoulder and jaw. Whom to call? I listen to the insistent dial tone as if it's a real connection, until the tone sounds a warning: the handset has been off the hook too long. As if I'm not there. Or here.

What to do about the origin of the gnarled root of the psychic emergency that happened decades ago but still sprouts like a frail sapling? An ER would be too loud, bright, large, busy at 3 a.m. on a hot Saturday night. Perhaps, instead, an emergency roomlette, a space the size of a closet complete with doctorettes, who prescribe pills so small it's impossible to overdose. They don't trust the patient with full-sized ones.

Moth wings beat-flutter the screen.
  What's out there?
  The past?

Sorrow, shrunk to the size of a dollhouse with miniature people whose miniature hearts are too faint to hear, as if listening through a child's plastic, make-believe phonelette.

If only the tangible smell of pine straw drifted across night: warm, almost acrid with August heat. But the scent is only a hintlette, too evanescent to inhale fully.

I fear some homunculus of remorse will always find me.

Homunculus because it looks small when seen from the outside, but inside it's mythically vast. Because grief conceals its vastness. No matter how hard you wad up a damp tissue, it retains the flood of tears your heartlette unleashed.

Psych Ward, Drought

On August 30, later that same summer in Georgia, it had not rained for two months. I lay on the green velvet Victorian couch like a frail pre–Civil War southern belle. Never mind that I was neither southern nor a belle but more or less a Yankee, out of her habitat, dressed in the same stained tank top and cut-off jeans.

Frail? A frail slut?

Regardless, with my future ex-husband in California on a research grant, this state of weather seemed insurmountable. No rain compounded by the inexorable sun. One more thing to endure. Or the last thing I was unable to endure.

I felt bereft.

And hot.

My fantasies ranged from cloudy skies to soft drops of water to a deluge of biblical proportions.

In the dryness—maybe I fantasized it, maybe I didn't—I heard random things cracking. Like coffee cups in the pantry. Egg shells in the refrigerator. Needles of loblollies. Legs of daddy longlegs. Strands of my hair. The top of my skull.

This was the final motivation I needed to drive to the psych ward at the local hospital on September 1. I'd had it.

Besides, surely, at least, the psych ward would be air-conditioned.

I was given paperwork, questions to answer: *Why are you here? Do you hear voices? Do you want to hurt yourself?*

Questions. To which there were no answers. Or maybe I no longer remembered the answers.

The intake nurse, eyes hard as a diagnosis, turned the key opening the unit, ushering me in. She locked the door behind us. She led me to a room.

I sat on an orange Naugahyde chair. I stared out the large window overlooking the parking lot, the unrelenting sky.

My outlook only seemed to change on the unit because I felt/feel myself shift from past tense to the immediacy of present.

As in: This *is* a mistake.

As in: A nurse encourages me to go to lunch. To group therapy. To art therapy.

As in: I refuse to leave my orange chair.

As in: Heat radiates off the asphalt parking lot, waves of it rippling across my eyes.

Of course I could say most of my life is a mistake: parents, boyfriends, lovers, husbands. To say nothing of my inability to do well in school. I have no steady employment. No interests. No hobbies. No children.

But today this is beside the point. All I want is rain.

By about four in the afternoon, still sitting on the chair—in this never-ending present—the orange now reminds me of the merciless sun that never softens. I decide to leave the locked unit without fully understanding the concept of "locked unit."

The hospital doesn't seem to understand the meaning of it either. Because when I step from my room, I notice the door to the unit is wide open. Maybe a nurse or an aide inadvertently neglected to close it.

I simply walk out. I enter the corridor and head toward the exit sign. I'm about halfway down the hall when a nurse calls my name, her rubber-soled shoes scuffing after me, ordering me back, that I have not been *discharged*.

"We'll call the police," she yells.

Good luck with that, I think.

I bolt for the exit. Slam into my car. Drive away.

That night, I stand in the field behind my house. The weeds are brittle and dry beneath my bare feet. The hard-bright stars crack the sky into pieces, a splintering that never seems to stop.

Expiration Date

I board the plane wearing an off-the-shoulder peasant dress I bought in Bascarsija, the bazaar in Sarajevo. It's bright yellow like a warning signal before switching to red, to *stop*. I wave goodbye to my boyfriend—is he still my boyfriend?—who will remain in Dubrovnik another week. But he's already turning away. Without waving.

I plop down beside an older man, my seatmate for the transatlantic flight. He wears a wedding ring. A three-piece suit and tie. A white pressed shirt.

The air-conditioning is cold. I slip off my leather sandals and wrap my feet in an airplane blanket.

Over dinner we engage in chit-chat: my job on Capitol Hill, my first after graduating college; his work in the import-export business. His wife, kids.

We soon run out of sunlight and small talk. Stars orient the sky. But I am consumed by the emptiness of space, the closeness of strangers. I whisper that my boyfriend and I had a fight. He asks what it was about.

How to explain the fight was, and wasn't, about my inability to provide directions as we drove from Split to Sarajevo to Montenegro to Dubrovnik? Lost in the middle of Bosnia, or was it Herzegovina, my boyfriend yelled at me for being, well, stupid. Unable to read or follow a map.

But *he* was the one I was unable to read. We'd dated for several years, and watching his intemperate, mistral eruptions, I wondered how I'd never seen him before. Or maybe he'd never seen me? *We* were directionless, lost on roads more byzantine than those through foreign terrain, on untranslatable gazettes or globes.

Yet now that I'm here on the plane, our fights seem to belong to another continent. To a different language. One I no longer speak.

The man, half-laughing, squeezes my hand and whispers that the best part of a relationship occurs during the first ten minutes.

When the man stirs beside me, midway across the Atlantic, I realize he's awakened from a nap. The yellow-red tip of the sun is lifting from the horizon. I remove the blanket that'd been warming my feet and spread it across his lap. I barely hear him unzip his slacks over the roar of engines.

I lean over.

Less than ten minutes.

Against Ruin

Is it the moment after my cat Quizzle dies, when a hummingbird rises up to the glass sliders, where Quizzle whispers away? Or is it the moment the man, a stranger, carries me on his back into the Caribbean to teach me to swim but touches me *there*, underwater, where no one can see? A touch so brief and insubstantial maybe it's the fin of a fish . . . Or the moment driving alone from Michigan to Galveston, running away from a husband, when headlights sweep cascading rain, the night, when I can barely see, can't see because I never know what I'm looking for? Or the moment I inhale a whiff of sawdust . . . and I enter the past, decades ago, my first childhood home on Southern Avenue in DC, my father building furniture in the living room, when planks of wood are transubstantiated into chairs, tables, bedframes? I still, even now, possess two of those chairs, moldering in my basement. Cobwebs bind them together as much as dowels and glue. I could clean them, buy new cushions. I don't. Nor can I part with them even though the now-dead father who built them was a bad man. Really, it's *all* these moments, coupled together, that cause me to realize that the things bequeathed or left behind, the totality of it, remain part of the scaffold holding me together.

Emerald Isle

St. Thomas, USVI

I hid on the verandah of our house on Blackbeard's Hill watching my parents' elegant parties. Mainly, I admired the crème de menthe, how it glittered in long-stemmed liqueur glasses, how women sipped it as evening approached midnight, shimmering like the gems on their bracelets, necklaces, earrings. But the crème de menthe was more engaging: a small sea offering green tides of joy.

Decades later, I still own one of my parents' crème de menthe bottles. I display it on a shelf in my Michigan kitchen. The slender neck balloons to a globe still half-filled. The distiller is Marie Brizard & Roger, Bordeaux, France, founded in the 1770s, still thriving. The faded label promotes it as a "liqueur hygenique & digestive."

Even before the cork cracked, before the liqueur turned, I never drank from it. Nor have I ordered crème de menthe in restaurants. It's too mystical, alluring, exquisite, resplendent. It's too consumed by adjectives. It must remain in glass globules to be admired, protected, savored like memory, like those rare moments when a tropical setting sun, in a flash, turns from sapphire yellow to emerald green.

After the party I inhaled the glasses' residue, which smelled cool as twilight rain on frangipani leaves.

Al Di Là

1.

Jamie is the first boy you notice when you start public school after moving from the West Indies to Glen Rock. He's not literally the first boy you see, but it feels as if he is. You sit alone in the cafeteria. Girls at the next table lean toward each other giggling. Outside, beyond a row of windows, you see New Jersey trees you can't name, no tropical palms or frangipanis. You feel wrong in your madras outfit. All the other girls wear pastel. It didn't occur to you to shop for new clothes: a mistake.

Now in seventh grade, Stateside, you feel suddenly (almost) sophisticated. Surely you'll be even more so once you buy new dresses and transform your long braid into a sleek French twist.

Jamie sits several tables away. You can't stop glancing at him. You're sure he embodies the essence of a suburban Bergen County boy. Blond hair. Cute pug nose. A pressed cotton shirt. He's joking with friends but not boisterously, almost quietly, as if he might be shy. If only he notices you, maybe you'll be conjured into an authentic Jersey girl.

You time your departure from the cafeteria in order to pass through the wide double doors together. He nods and smiles, his front teeth slightly crooked, which you love. The backs of your knees feel tender with longing. You pause to watch him walk down the corridor to his next class. You feel unreal. Have you landed in a movie—as if a camera, a long-shot, pans his image until he turns the corner? *Is this a film of your first love . . . love at first sight?*

2.

After dating Jamie a few months, the two of you see the movie *Rome Adventure* starring Troy Donahue and Suzanne Pleshette. In the darkened theater, you in your pale pink cotton shirtwaist, your arm grazes Jamie's. He doesn't respond. In this overly romantic movie, the two protagonists break up but reunite, in movie time, *forever*.

Here in the present, now hovering, as you are, inside literary time, you know how your own film ends. It is only back then, in the past, that you yearned for Jamie to be bewitched by the protagonists, to mimic them, to love you year after year, too.

The origin of the word "melodrama" is rooted in *melos*, or music, honey.

Jamie is music and honey. You provide the drama, certain that no one else in the universe has experienced love's ecstatic existence or its heartrending absence, which you'll feel in a few months when he leaves you.

But for now, in the movie, Donahue and Pleshette are sophisticated and beautiful. Perfect. They sit at an outdoor café sipping Strega, the color of a Hollywood sun.

What says "love" more than outdoor cafés in Rome, Strega liqueur, and lingering glances?

In the theater, Jamie and you sip 7-Up and eat popcorn. Jamie smells of both, sugar and salt, or what you think of as "suburban boy." Maybe you dabbed your wrists with Canoe. Your hair is either in a flip or a French twist. Who can remember exactly? Either way, it's rigid with Aqua Net.

But wait...

In that moment, you're convinced *you* are drinking Strega. How can Jamie fail to taste it, too? He is, after all, watching the same movie.

Surely, together, you both can be magical as the magic of the silver screen.

In the movie Suzanne Pleshette says, *Life is about the need to be loved.*

The film, based on the novel *Lovers Must Learn*, features the song "Al Di Là." Loosely translated it means "far, far away," or "beyond the beyond . . . beyond this world," or how much the singer, Emilio Pericoli, loves his beloved. And by extension, how much Donahue and Pleshette love each other.

And by further extension, how much you want Jamie to love you, as surely you love him.

In real life, Suzanne Pleshette and Troy Donahue marry, but they divorce after eight months.

Lovers *must* learn. All you learn as a teen is what you see in *Rome Adventure*. You pin all your hopes on "beyond the beyond." You pin your entire relationship, actual *existence*, on *Rome Adventure*. The outcome of the movie, you convince yourself, must be your outcome with Jamie. *Al Di Là!*

After the movie, standing under the marquee, you ask Jamie what he thought of it.

"It was good," he says.

3.

Strega is the Italian word for "witch," though you prefer another interpretation: "sorceress." Ancient myth claims that, on Saturday nights, a coven danced on the banks of the River Sabato and brewed a potion to ensure everlasting love for all couples who drank it.

If only you offered Strega to Jamie, its notes of star anise, saffron, mint. Surely more potent than 7-Up.

4.

Decades later, you re-watch the movie on Amazon Prime. Afterward, you stand by the window in your bedroom, "Al Di Là" playing in your mind like a soundtrack. The moon swoons low in the sky, the summer street deserted. You want to stand on a balcony overlooking the Trevi Fountain. You want to re-create that moment in the theater, sitting beside Jamie, watching the film together, your arms almost touching. You wanted Jamie to hold your hand when Troy held Suzanne's. When Troy kissed Suzanne, you leaned closer to Jamie, trying to will him to kiss you, too. You wanted to embrace moments of music, of honey, of saffron, of drama—to understand love before all slipped beyond the beyond.

Driving home from the theater that night, you and Jamie do not pass the Colosseum, the Pantheon, the Trevi Fountain on a Vespa. In a red Rambler, you pass Gilroy's Market, Mandee's Dress Shop, a deserted main street, the faint scent of sugar from the Nabisco factory on the outskirts of town.

Into the Wild of the Calm

I stand at a nighttime window in my home in Michigan watching two deer sleep in my snowy yard, enclosed by fences and heavy foliage meant to keep them out. Yet here they are. I want to don my parka as if it's fur and curl up beside them. Will they accept me into their herd? Where will we hoof in the blue light of dawn? I leave behind teacups, spoons, photos of nameless ancestors, books whose words I no longer remember, shed hair, mismatched socks, memories, *dejected membra*, scattered fragments, in order to enter the scent of evergreen, the flick of dune grass, the lap of waves along the lakeshore, the quiet of snow, the exuberance of stars. I pound my hooves casting open the untethered, the un-reined, the unseen windows of other lives.

The Lost Art of the Near Tilt

Drunk, in the Moulin Rouge in Galveston, alone at a Pac-Man table, sipping Snake River Stampede whisky, I decide I want a divorce. In truth, I never proactively wanted to marry. In spite of myself, I left my job on Capitol Hill to move to Texas with my first husband. *As a bride.* So this night, my husband out of town, the decision clarifies.

After all, I'm racking up a great score.

After all, the night swirls with a neon jukebox twanging "Rhinestone Cowboy," the foosball thwacking, couples two-stepping on the small dance floor, cigarette smoke curling. The bar and logic hazing.

Pac-Man glides through the maze gobbling dots. Meanwhile, a red ghost sweeps along tunnels trying to swallow him. *Eat or be eaten.* I feed quarters into the slot, mesmerized by the mindless yet high-stakes game of survival. Fight or flight.

///

No man would have lasted, anyway. I was "dating" three men at once when I tossed a coin, shrugged, and decided on *this* one to marry. I left the others in the dust. But the ring hadn't yet wedded my finger before I was gazing ahead to where I might land next.

Since birds are descended from dinosaurs, I might land with the *whomp* of a T-Rex, or gently as a goldfinch.

///

As "Stand by Your Man" (unlikely) plays on the jukebox, I amble over to the Pistol Poker pinball machine. Cowboys, jail cells, cacti, rattlesnakes, girls in bikini tops illuminate the board. I lean against it in my cut-off jeans and off-the-shoulder t-shirt. I pull the plunger. A silver ball spits from the chute. Lights flash. *Clang-clanging* echoes. Bells ding. A tinny *hee-haw* competes with the jukebox. The ball bounces off targets, careens along Black Jack Ramp. It zings around bumpers, kickers, slingshots. I snap the flippers. The ball boomerangs up to the top. My score rises. I have enough quarters stashed in my pocket for the balls to zoom away to their ultimate fate almost all night.

Unlike Pac-Man, a pinball machine lets you bump against it to help elevate your score. Hit it too hard, however, you tilt it. End of game. I know just how much I can cheat before it catches up with me. Or so I want to believe.

///

How best to survive the night? Order another Snake River Stampede? Stare out the salt-stained plate-glass window at ghostly images of the Seawall and Gulf superimposed on the bar's boozy scene? Bump up against a strange man?

///

Maybe Pac-Man is Darwin's theory of evolution in microcosm, or the theory of evolution-as-experiment in one sweaty, smudgy, smutty honkytonk bar. Where sometimes you win, other times a whole species—or just you—vanishes. Into thin air. Into night.

In a couple of years Pac-Man will evolve into Ms. Pac-Man with new music, different sound effects, and a heroine who must fly even faster, so her ghosts don't consume her one pixel, one regret, one life at a time.

The Origin of Her Superpowers

One evening, the world lit by a moon the color of parchment, the girl walks past the town's swimming pool and finds a velvet worm. It's as if the worm wants to be noticed by donning a red-and-gold velvet robe just for her. The girl realizes that the worm has misunderstood: it can't drink from the chlorinated pool. It needs the girl to offer pure nourishment, as much as the girl needs the worm, for reasons soon to be clear. She carries the worm home where she lives with her parents and sister. She builds a nest for it from bobby pins and a hairnet. She places a cotton ball on the bottom along with a thimbleful of water. She pops the worm inside.

On the girl's walk, she found other creatures she could have adopted: turtles, cow sharks, horseshoe crabs, gray egrets, and crocodiles. All creatures millions of years old. Creatures who already survived drought, fires, floods, blight, plagues, pandemics.

The girl loves the velvet worm best.

The girl keeps it within easy reach, knowing she'll need it at a moment's notice. It tells the girl about its properties developed over a span of 500 million years. It has limbs on either side of its head that convert into slime guns. These twin streams of slime are strong enough to immobilize its prey. Once it touches the target its chaotic protein hardens immediately and is always fatal. It feeds only at night.

Over the weeks, the girl studies the velvet worm. Turning on a small flashlight, she crouches beside her bed and watches how it maneuvers—its speed and precision—whenever a fly, spider, or mosquito enters its home.

The worm is an excellent teacher. Finally, the girl is ready.

The next time the girl's father opens the door to her room late at night, while her mother and sister sleep, she and the velvet worm move into position. How else to survive, to not go extinct?

Her own arms rise. Take aim. Shoot.

Miss Demeanor Must Consider, Whether She Wants to or Not, the Time Awaiting the Crucifixion When the Via Dolorosa Was the Sorrowful Southern Avenue in Washington DC, Only Nine Steps across the Sepulcher While Nailed on a Couch

Father, fumbling buttons.
Girl's arm, hand, reaching out for safety.
Who's the guilty photographer?

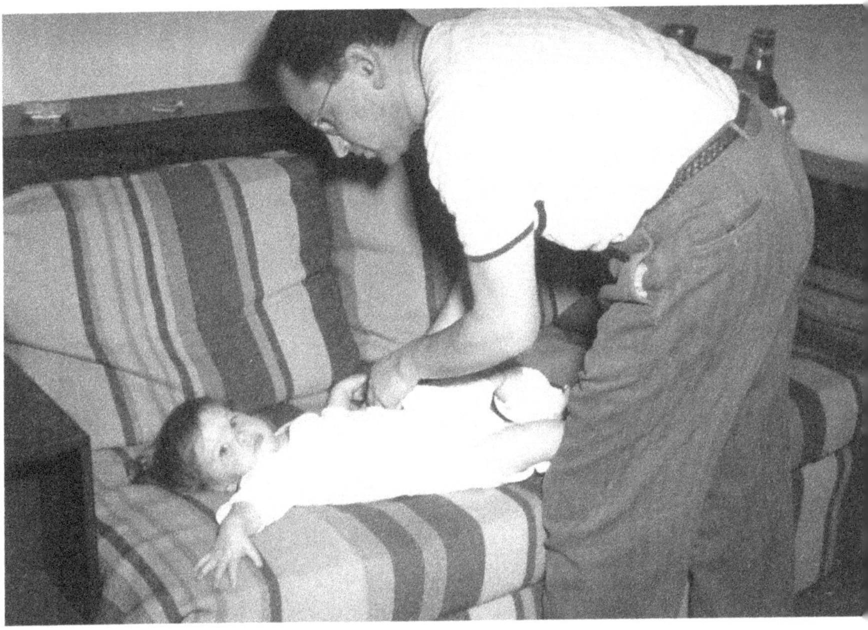

Miss Demeanor Must Also Consider the Time Her Father Took This Illicit Pre-Teen Snapshot of Her in the Dining Room of the Suburban Ranch in Glen Rock, New Jersey, Only the Modigliani Woman Watching

Eyes, illegal.
Eyes, wary.
Eyes see what they see, know what they know.

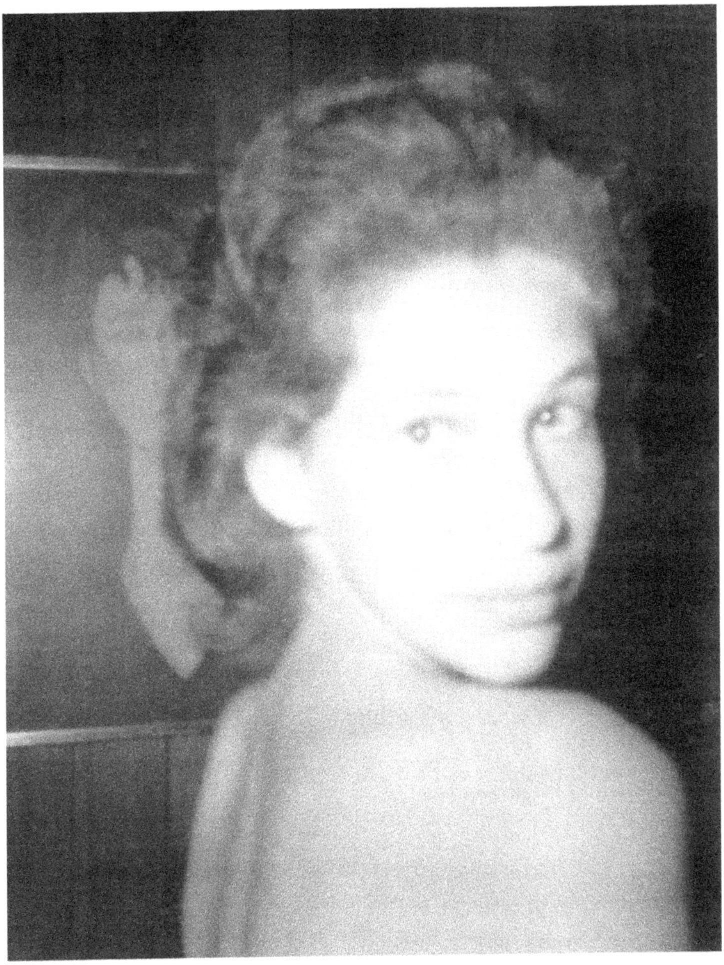

Tinea Capitis

> The oldest decipherable full sentence in an alphabet ever found, dated to 1,700 B.C.E., is inscribed on a tiny ivory comb unearthed in 2016 at the Tel Lachish archeological site in central Israel. The faint letters read: "May this tusk root out the lice of the hair and the beard."
> —Sarah Cascone, artnet.com

Joey, a toddler, sits on my lap on the porch steps of the orphanage. I stayed late to help feed the kids their dinner. I stayed late because Joey clung to me. I stayed late because, though I didn't fully know it then, I will never have my own children. Maybe I suspect as much. I also suspect I'm at a loss to convey such a singular moment, to fully translate experience to narrative. A flash in time. When nothing, exactly, happens. Maybe this evening with Joey would sound more introspective in Latin. For example, "I will never have children" is *Et filios non habere*. At least according to the online translator—not in existence back then—though Latin, of course, was. But it, too, is one of many things I never learned, *didicit*. Or any other ancient language.

Joey and I are half-cast in shadow from the dim orphanage lights. Still, the small red tracks circling his shaved scalp, like a tattoo, are visible. If it weren't for the pustules I would rest my chin on his head, tuck him against me more tightly. I don't. Well, I hug him, but I avoid what the doctor calls *tinea capitis*, which sounds almost elegant, as opposed to the English "ringworm of the scalp." I imagine each scale hard as plaque. Whether contagious or not, I fear an infection deeper than skin. Or *leprae humiliorem cute timeo*.

Do the words "abandoned," "illness," and "lost" sound less forsaken in Latin?

As a temporary high school summer employee, here in New Jersey, I'm not allowed to read all of Joey's history. In a locative declension, however, I know his parents abandoned him *at* the orphanage, where, datively speaking, the orphanage received him. It's uncertain if one or both will reclaim him. It's uncertain whether anyone will claim him—*ut sis facis.*

I also stayed late at the orphanage to eat with the kids in order to avoid dinner with my parents. Avoid my father's rage if the food isn't cooked correctly. Avoid my mother's sour silence. Avoid my sister's empty chair, now *always* empty, since she left for college. Avoid my own place at the dining room table, only a silent girl in my family's rigid, untranslatable roles. I'm the girl who exists, *est*, between the way my father massages my shoulders after dinner and the way my mother pretends not to notice. But now, I wonder, if called *puella*, not girl, is a different outcome possible?

As night, *noctis*, deepens, I point out stars to Joey, not that I myself can identify constellations any more than I know Latin. But just to be speaking to him, I whisper, *Aries, Cancer, Gemini, Aquarius, Leo, Taurus, Scorpio, Virgo, Libra, Pisces, Sagittarius, Capricorn.*

I tell Joey I'm an Aries. I don't know Joey's sign of the Zodiac.

I want to give him a *signum* as if I can anoint him with a specific meaning. I want him to be a solid, tangible boy that someone will see and want, someone will translate into *puer meus es tu.* You are my boy.

Joey doesn't respond to my poorly expressed explanation of patterns in the sky. Besides, the stars seem hard as glitter: *quasi fulgor stellae difficile.* In their shiny distance it seems as if you could slip on stars across the sky, across night, and never find your way home, *domum.*

I pull Joey closer. I press a fingertip against what feels like a scab. I trace another. I want the sores to alight like his own *constellatio* as if either the *magicae et stellas* or Latin will save him. But I fear they are an outer manifestation of deeper wounds—of the soul, of the body—of *tinea capitis*, for which there is no cure or graceful translation or happy conclusion.

Non est remedium, vel translatione vel graceful optatum exitum deducatur.

Or is there?

Aut est ibi?

After that summer I never see Joey again.

Quid accidit?

How can you know what happens?

A Grand Unified Theory of Disease

When my great-aunt visits smelling of cloves, oranges, and sulfur, I hide in my bedroom closet in our DC duplex until my parents force me out. I stand before her, on an Oriental rug, wishing I could sink into it, could disguise myself in its arabesque design. She beams at me. She bends to kiss me. But all I see, nearing me, is a bulge of skin quivering from her neck.

After she leaves, this growth haunts me. I'm only in first grade so the word "goiter" means nothing. To me, it is a sign, a hex, a contagion. I'm terrified I'll inherit it.

It's as if my great-aunt staggers through life with the world's sins sagging from her neck.

Does the goiter scare *her*? Depress *her*? What about her clove, orange, sulfur? Who *is* my aunt? Who would she be without her goiter? For all I know maybe, without it, she'd feel lonely, ordinary.

Over the years, after we move to St. Thomas, then New Jersey, and beyond, I forget about my great-aunt's goiter. I only consider it again when, in 2020, I contract (inherit?) a mild case of pneumonia. I undergo X-rays and CT scans, photos of the inside of my body, bacteria settling into sacs. These prokaryotes are cells lacking a nucleus. Does this mean, after invading the organism, they float through pores into my lungs? When the pneumonia subsides, my lungs continue to expel liquid like wavelets emptying the ocean of my afflicted soul.

More than the pneumonia and its residue, I worry about all my organs. I worry about each blood cell—red, white, platelets, plasma—and any system failure that could occur either with or without warning. While medical reasons exist why one person gets a goiter and another pneumonia, what does the body itself want us to know? Can the body, all on its own, attempt suicide-by-disease?

After all, the brain, on its own, can decide to make the body sick. Psychosomatic illness isn't fake, isn't illness "just in your mind." The brain convinces the body to decline. But since they aren't separate, the mind and body, along with the soul, conspire to present new and undiagnosable maladies.

For example, if the soul is depressed, the body might respond with an ailment that eludes diagnosis and treatment. And if the body is physically depleted, it often causes the mind to lose hope and the soul to lose faith.

My pulmonologist can't explain how I got pneumonia, though it wasn't from another person. During the pandemic, I've been quarantining.

I study the X-ray, my lungs a ghostly outline surrounded by a void. Hunkered in the right lobe is a clot of disease. Lungs, I want to ask you: *Why are you sick? Are you sad? Dismayed? Scared? Are you tired of breathing, exhausted by that constant flutter-flutter-flutter? What can I do to make you happy, or at least satisfied enough to perform your job?*

If I lived inside an MRI machine, I would know the exact location—time and place—of the pneumonia's attack. Safely cocooned inside a round cylinder, I could monitor constant images of my insides. I, as organism, would have up-to-date notifications on all my body's goings-on. The machine's whir, negating harsh sounds of the outside world, would soothe me. The machine would know, at any given moment, who I am and when I should be on high alert.

Upon further consideration, however, my MRI machine would need to be outfitted with gadgets to also observe soulful feelings and emotions. Sadly, that machine must still be a prototype, or on the drawing board.

Except, when the latest CT scan results arrive, I read words such as "occult," "mosaic attenuation," "no ground-glass opacity," "partial halo." Such mystical phrases to describe my lungs. Or me?

Maybe my great-aunt suffered melancholia, a well of loss too profound to speak. That's why scientific knowledge does not erase my fear of her goiter. Even though doctors claim a goiter is caused by lack of iodine in the diet, I believe, even if she swallowed a box of salt, her goiter would not have shrunk. If you sprinkled all the iodized salt in the world—salted the entire earth—the malevolence I perceived in her goiter would still contaminate those with immune-suppressed emotions.

Surely there's a metaphysical connection between my aunt's goiter and that indentation in the forehead of my college physics professor. When I visited him in his office that afternoon after class, when I sat on his lap hoping to improve my grade, he slid his hand up my thigh under my green-plaid miniskirt. Initially, I was failing physics because I was overwhelmed by what I did and didn't know about antimatter. But I clearly felt that gamma-ray electrical charge of *his* matter . . . felt his buzz-cut hair scratch my face.

Only now I recall that I opened my eyes when he kissed me, focusing on the gouge in his forehead. Was it a groove from a surgically removed melanoma? Was the depression in his forehead a, well, *depression*, an outward manifestation of sadness caused by his own absent matter, a wound so deep it was like missing vital organs?

At the same time, as he neared me, as when my aunt's goiter drew closer, I felt almost paralyzed by the sheer scope of what could befall the human body. I couldn't look at it; I couldn't gaze away.

Maybe the solution is that I (all of us) need one diagnosis that considers the mind and body as one entity. In fact, I'd welcome such a label; just give me one that's inclusive. I don't want to say I have a headache. Or pneumonia. Or appendicitis. Or depression. I want a classification for the entire organism. Brand me "Blue." Or "Snow." Or the scent of hyacinths. The rough bark of a magnolia or pine. Mark me "haloed in a mosaic occult." Categorize me "inoperatively melancholy" or "ground-glass pissed."

I've been called borderline personality, obsessive, an abandoned woman, a sufferer of intermittent IBS. You see the problem? All, and more, are true. I am a constellation of disorders. Therefore, I need an overriding label that speaks for the whole.

Existence depends on such inclusivity. Without one, I am a stranger to myself.

The physics professor must be a misogynist in that he seduced a young student. But what about his melanoma? If he had one definitive classification maybe the seduction would not have happened. Maybe his teleology would have been clear. Clearer. Known. I could classify him a Melanoma for Wounded Women, although I do not think that term would cure him.

Maybe we are all wounded because, lacking our own special mark, we are displaced, dispossessed strangers to ourselves and to each other. Am I the same as everyone else suffering depression or pneumonia? Surely, my own suffering is unique. Can I trademark it?

A goiter is caused by lack of salt or an inflammation of the thyroid. Pneumonia is caused by bacteria or virus. The physics professor's indentation presented as a melanoma when my gaze fixated on it, my pupils dilated. Other things are caused by sin or karma or bad luck.

If that's what you believe.

I do; I don't.

Do I want a diagnosis or prognosis? Do I want to know the cause or the outcome, the effect? Both. I want an all-encompassing theory to give comfort and understanding. Otherwise, how do we survive, how do we live, each of us, with our own private brands of hope and grief?

Organ Music

I sit on a stool in the radiology department at Spectrum Health in Grand Haven, Michigan, about five minutes from home. I am alone in a deserted hallway of white tiles and waxed floors waiting my turn. A week ago, a CT scan, to ensure my lungs are clear of the pneumonia I had months ago (they are), stumbled upon a "questionable soft tissue fullness in the region of the pancreatic tail. Probable left renal cyst." Now I'm back for an MRI of my pancreas. Is this tissue benign? Malignant? An innocent smudge on the CT screen? A stray piece of undigested food that bypassed the head and body of the pancreas to perch on its tail?

Who really knows how parts of the body work? And how long has my pancreas been ailing? This discovery is a fluke.

Of course I've endlessly Googled it. The pancreas converts food into fuel for the body's cells. Its exocrine function assists digestion; its endocrine function regulates blood sugar. It's spongy, shaped like a flat pear. The origin of the word suggests "sweetbread" or "raw flesh." In fact, if you've ever eaten sweetbread, you've eaten the pancreas of a lamb. *Exactly.*

But I want to know about my specific pancreas. As if Google itself can be an MRI machine whereby, from the comfort of your home, every morning upon waking, you perform an easy full-body check. Just stick a body part into your computer and, instantaneously, a message flashes on the screen. *Benign. Malignant. Broken. Splintered. Fractured. Watch out! Warning! Heartbreak! Calamity! Ruin! Recheck in a year.*

When you turn on the engine of a car, after all, the dashboard alights signaling the amount of gas in the tank. Whether the engine is low on oil. Brake and wiper fluid. Air pressure in the tires. If your car signals a low battery charge, the mechanic easily replaces it. I, too, want flashing lights, warning signs, for each body part. For example, if I need new valves or arteries simply pop my hood and insert them. As simple as overhauling a malfunctioning machine until it's a well-maintained happy mechanism. Or, even better, I want an "all clear" sign without having to wait a week for test results.

For now, alone in the radiology corridor, I wear a hospital gown, tied at the back, and pant scrubs. Both are many sizes too large, and my body feels diminished, as if it's wasting away without a properly operating pancreas. I am allowed to wear my beret, my hair tucked inside, along with a mask to protect me from COVID.

Behind me, in a control room, two technicians speak into a microphone to the person currently in the MRI machine. I feel, more than hear, its low vibration behind the wall. I wonder about the person inside it. Which organ troubles them? Which one is discordant?

An elderly man finally emerges. He shuffles past me in thin slippers returning to the locker room to change into his clothes. The back of his gown gapes open. His torso is dotted with large moles. They look suspicious. I consider offering him the name of my dermatologist. But possibly he has a more significant issue (brain can't think; stomach can't digest; heart can't feel or even pump blood) looming beneath his skin.

Issues that give him about ten minutes left to live.

Like me?

Two technicians bundle me onto the narrow slab, preparing to roll me into the MRI. They place a pillow under my head. Wedges under my arms. A plastic girdle across my abdomen. I'm given a rubber ball to squeeze that emits a sound if I need to get their attention once the test begins. *Do you want to listen to music?* they ask. I draw a blank. What kind of music could I possibly request? Golden oldies from the 1960s? Would my pancreas rock 'n' roll to the beat of "I Wanna Hold Your Hand"? *A pancreas doesn't have hands.* Or could I listen to twangy country-western guitars, lyrics wailing about lost love, abandonment, melodrama? But I generate enough of my own. I try to imagine my pancreas wearing a western hat and cowboy boots. Classical music might be a safer bet, but will the MRI last long enough to reach the end, say, of Mozart's "Requiem in D Minor," a work cut short by the composer's death? Since the MRI will be photographing my entire torso—kidneys, liver, bladder, the whole shebang—it could be a veritable organ recital. Starring, of course, the pancreas. But my pancreas doesn't want the spotlight. It wants to hide in the wings. And who could blame it? Any sane pancreas must absolutely regret being conceived, and forced to live, in an entity (person, mind, body) that's such an always-expect-the-worst-depressed-downer drama queen as I.

I shake my head at the technicians. No music. Besides my inability to select the right genre, music is designed to bring you out of yourself. I am too sunk inside myself. I want to be able to whisper, to soothe my one scared pancreas. Does my pancreas itself know if it's ailing? Maybe it knows but simply lacks the ability to communicate its findings, its fate, to me.

Despite my no-music request, the technicians clamp a headset over my ears so they can explain procedures from their control room. They shut the heavy door. I'm not afraid of confined spaces. I'm not claustrophobic. In fact, I like to be cocooned inside this round hollow space, unseen, distant from the outside world. As if unseen is safety, a place no one can find me. Disease can't find me (unless the malady already sprouts inside me). Even the technicians' voices sound tinny, distant, as if originating from outer space. They tell me when and how to breathe. When to hold my breath. The MRI machine itself speaks more distinctly. With every image it snaps, it clanks, rattles, whirs, growls. The noises remind me of a bowling alley, the thud-drop of neon-colored balls skittering down a slick surface. About halfway through, the MRI sounds as if it's speaking in tongues: low moans follow a series of high-pitched shrieks. Or it's as if two people are engaged in an argument, debating the fate of my pancreas. I attempt to decipher the language, whether one sound means its X-ray vision detects malignant wounds while the other signals A-OK.

Dearest Pancreas,

Please be on your best behavior. Please glow rosy clear and unblemished. I love you and promise to do everything possible to take good care of you.

Your grateful host,
Sue xo

I consider my little-girl body, once shiny and new. Sure, one has to grow, but why can't one's organs remain intact, simply slide, without change or incident, through childhood, into adolescence, adulthood, and beyond? And while I'm thinking of it, why can't our feelings, our emotions, be likewise suspended with the unknowledgeable knowledge of an infant before, well, we fuck everything up into an existential miasma?

If only I were born inside this MRI womb and remained suspended in its constant monitoring of all my body's moving parts.

I check My Chart numerous times a day for the results. When, finally, they appear it's almost anti-climactic. That formation initially revealed on the CT scan is merely an undramatic "benign anatomical variant. The pancreatic parenchymal signal and enhancement is normal and homogeneous. No pancreatic lesions presented. No pancreatic inflammation or edema."

Not that I understand all the words in the medical report. Nor do I need to. As a savant organist, I play everything inside me by ear.

Dyscalculia

a learning disorder affecting a person's ability to do basic math

1 delusional father = 0 father
1 depressed + emotionally deranged mother = 0 mother
1 absent sister = 0 sister
Which, if you can follow the logic, minus 0 family = 1,757,000 feelings of abandonment (do the math)

2 dead dogs = 2 once-alive dogs = 2 badly trained dogs = 0 dog companionship

4 dead cats = 4 once-alive cats =
    1: the creature love of my life
    1: agoraphobic
    1: self-righteous = Republican tendencies
    1: meek + downtrodden = Democratic tendencies

1 mini-fire, deliberately set = wanting to burn the house down in 9th grade but failing = 0 satisfying fires

6 years of elementary school = 214 years of being a lost educational cause
6 years of junior + senior high school = 666 additional years of being a lost cause = who cares about textbooks when 1,476 more interesting things happen daily outside of classrooms

5,875 books read = 12,364 pretend lives lived in lieu of my own 1 sorry life

375 friends lost along the way, but 5,000 friends on Facebook, which = something

22 houses + apartments = stray socks, buttons, shed hair left behind = loss

945 sordid motel rooms = X number sordid, shady, disturbed, temporarily ravenous men = 1 broken heart X number of times + quasi-mended, still = 1 soiled heart

1 body − 1 appendix = 1 almost whole body but more like 99% of a body

78,624 hours spent waiting for X, Y, Z to happen = 1,253,784 wasted hours of a finite life

4,274 meals missed = 1 anorexic body spanning 7 years

1 therapist who fired me + 1 therapist who helped me + 1 therapist who almost destroyed me = another 12 ineffectual therapists, leaving my questionable mental health in the red column

5,987 pairs of shoes mostly red

Wide Sargasso Sea + *The Notebooks of Malte Laurids Brigge* + *The Lover* + *Cane* + *The Collected Poetry of Lynda Hull* = top favorite books

Mystery Science Theater 3000 + *Twin Peaks* + *Moonlighting* = top TV shows

1 Maytag washing machine born circa 1989
3 clothes dryers

8,467 Xanax + Klonopin = the avoidance of 192,031 nervous breakdowns, still resulting in anywhere between 6 and 7 nervous breakdowns

45 CT scans + 76 X-rays + 33 MRIS = 1 hypochondriac
9 midnight trips to the ER, but that's conservative in the desire department because I'd like a suite attached to an ER for 24/7 care

173 dead-end jobs = 1 epiphany = 1 decision to attend graduate school = 12 years writing 5 (or 6) unpublishable novels = patience = 31,001 trees destroyed by all the both good and bad words I've written on paper

All = the story of 1 life.

POSTCARD   ***The Big Apple!***

Dear Future Me,

Here we are in NYC, all gritty streets and smelly subways, since Mom is too cheap to take taxis.

In Times Square, Mom and Dad rush Sis and me past all those peep shows and marquees advertising X-rated movies.

Everyone in the family wraps themselves in their own minor rage. Dad wants to take the Staten Island Ferry. Mom wants to visit museums. I want to lie in bed in the hotel room reading. Sis just wants to be rid of all of us and sneak away on her own. Fun times!

Love,
Sue

POSTCARD   *New York City*   PLACE
                                                    STAMP
Dear Future Me,   HERE

Still here. I find one thing I love: the Horn & Hardart automat. Cheap Mom is happy to give me a bunch of nickels for inexpensive food. I wander the wall of small rectangular windows spying hamburgers, mac and cheese, Salisbury steak, puddings. And slices of pie!! I crave one of everything simply for the thrill of sliding a nickel in the slot. Turning the knob. Opening the window. Everything in its own little container. Just like each member of my family.

Wish you were here!

Love,
Sue

Xeroxing Christie

I've had a crush on two women, but one was the actor Debra Winger. Which doesn't count. Yet listen to her voice: dark honey glistening on shattered glass. Like that.

If only . . .

The other, named Christie, according to her nametag, was a young woman who worked in the stationery store where I once Xeroxed terrible novels I wrote. *If only they were good.* At the time I didn't know they were terrible.

Pre-computer, I used a portable Smith-Corona typewriter, the color of burnt orange. But *if* I'd had a computer and printer, I would never have seen Christie.

She had silky orange hair. Well, not really. I'm desperately seeking connections among writing, typewriters, and her. Or the color orange. (You can see why the novels were terrible! I don't know how to make shit up.) Her hair, in reality, was pale-pale strawberry blonde.

She sat by a plate-glass window. The sun sparked her hair gold. That's not true, either.

But *if* she *had* sat by the window, her hair *would* have sparked gold. In reality, she sat far away from the window.

It took me over an hour to Xerox the three hundred or so pages of each bad novel. Over the course of several years, I wrote about five novels altogether. Back then you had to manually put one piece of paper in the machine at a time. I didn't mind.

I watched her sorting invoices, talking on the phone, signing orders. Sometimes she worked the cash register. Then, I tried to Xerox faster to stand close to her to pay.

She once asked me what I was Xeroxing, those mounds of paper killing all the loblollies in North Georgia, where I lived at the time. I told her I was a writer, that these were novels.

She didn't know how to respond. She giggled and seemed flustered. I was flustered as well because I wasn't exactly a writer. As Truman Capote said of Jack Kerouac: *That isn't writing, it's just typewriting.*

After that day Christie avoided me. Previously, if she met my gaze while I stood at the Xerox machine, she at her desk, we smiled. Now she never glanced at me.

Maybe she thought I was full of myself calling myself a writer. Maybe she was right. Maybe *she* thought, *I* thought I was more than she, since she clerked in a stationery store. The opposite was true.

I wasn't sure why I had a crush on her. Maybe it was her hair. Maybe it was the pale-pale skin of her arms in her sleeveless blouse when she swept her hair over her shoulder, almost unconsciously, as she focused on the work on her desk.

Maybe that crush removes some of the sting of all the years I wrote bad novels back then—and when I write about her now.

Miss Demeanor Considers the Time She Got Her First Author Photo, "Lay Lady Lay" Playing on the Radio, Except the Publisher Proclaimed the Visage Too Disturbing to Use

The sweater soft pink.
The hair wild, uncontrollable.
Eyes that never look away.

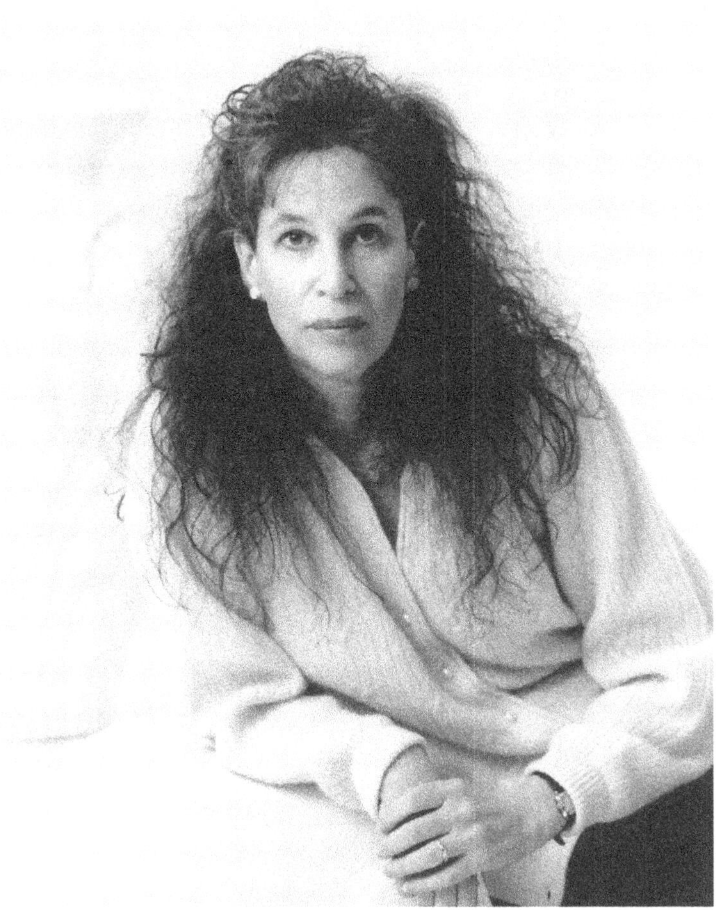

Miss Demeanor Considers Her Desk (Messy Like Her Life), in Her Own House, with a 1969 Edition of the *American Heritage Dictionary*, Taped Together—Still Indispensable—Also Like Her Life

Furniture inherited as well as assemble-it-yourself.
Room cluttered as her heart.
The room—her own.

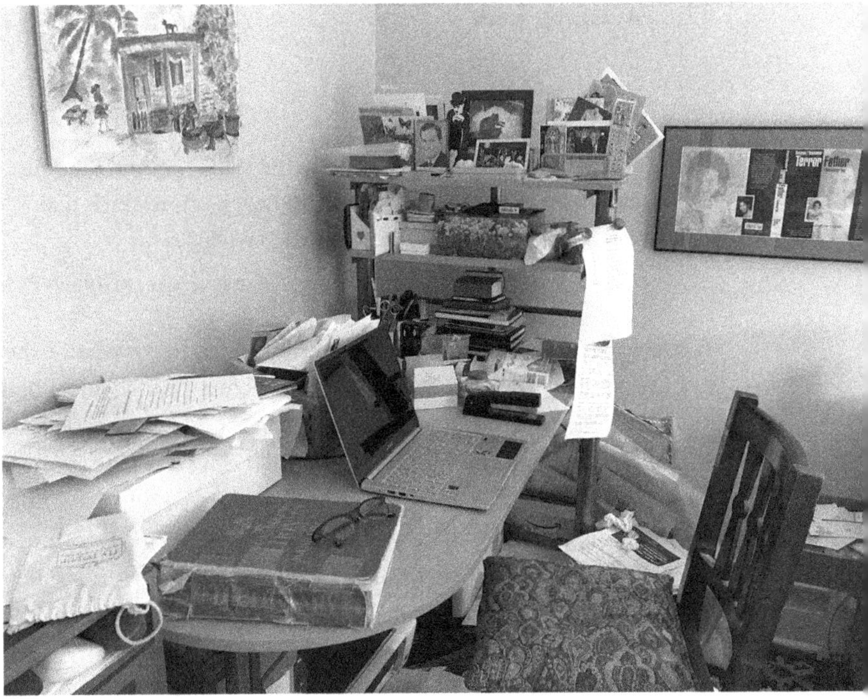

The Memory Box

> The past is hidden somewhere outside the realm, beyond the reach of intellect, in some material object (in the sensation which that material object will give us) which we do not suspect.
>
> —Marcel Proust, *Remembrance of Things Past*

A puzzle box, which my father brought me from Japan when I was a child, adorns my desk. It's three by two inches, an inch and a half high. Over the years the paint faded, but the picture remains: a house, with a pink roof and yellow and green walls, hovers on the shore of a lake. No windows. A gingko tree leans over it, while a junk boat is tied at the shoreline. A yellow sail with pink stripes arises from a pink deck. In the distance looms a snow-capped mountain.

Surrounding the picture, like a frame, are imbricated squares of pink, green, and yellow. Is the frame meant to resemble that of a window? Is the box itself meant to be a view from a window? Am I supposed to be gazing out a theoretical window *at* this view? Why does the house itself, mysteriously, lack windows? Is the true puzzle hidden inside *it*, the box, or inside the house?

My childhood home was a house with many windows, yet no one saw inside.

When I first receive the puzzle box, I spend over an hour figuring out how to open it. I finally find a panel camouflaged in the design on the side. I slide it back. Behind it hides a carved wooden knob. I push it. The box snaps open.

 I gasp. It's empty.

At that moment, I'm sitting on the floor of our house in Bethesda, Maryland. My sister, walking past, asks what's wrong.

I explain.

She laughs and says, "*You're* supposed to fill it." The owner of the box supplies the secret treasures to hide inside.

I'm only in second grade. What secret treasures could I possibly possess?

Is the box meant for tangible treasures or, given its smallness, intangible ones? As intangible as a memory. A secret.

Perhaps I consider: the silver key to my roller skates, my pink-and-white beaded birth bracelet, gardenia perfume, my Pluto the Dog hankie, canceled foreign stamps, dead leaves the texture of moth wings, the question marks of my shorn curls, winter dusk the color of the skin of plums, an ochre-colored bruise on my arm, my mother's tears, the red tinge on my father's cheeks when he's enraged, the sound of my sister's footsteps walking away from me.

In the living room, I gaze out the large plate-glass windows: our yard, with a small copse beyond. No one, of course, stands in the yard to glance inside. No one sees my angry father, my sad mother, my lost sister. An empty "me."

Who am I?

That windowless house seems to be more (less?) than a house lacking windows, just like the box feels like more (less?) than an empty gift.

I never, over the years, place any tangible mementos inside. Isn't it really designed to hoard memories? Or maybe words that create them.

This faded box on my desk is now broken. The drawer won't close. After all these years the interior spring mechanism has snapped. My own interior spring mechanism also, over time, snapped. Not a bad thing. If I hadn't broken open, I wouldn't have released the trove of memory-words inside.

Seeking Paradise on the Road to Nowhere

After I drive south from Grand Haven to Holland, Michigan, in my gold Toyota RAV, I turn onto Chicago Drive, which eventually becomes Eighty-Fourth Street. I feel as if I'm sinking into a portal of endlessness. Or as if a cumulonimbus descends from the sky, smothering me. I pass yellow brick houses with red trim, cottages with aluminum siding, small farms, barns, silos, out buildings—all spaced far apart, isolated. Whether I pass structures, fields, or stands of trees, there's a stifling sameness to the rural scenery. Nothing is ugly. Rather, I sense desolation and, in this desolation, an existential dread.

After only a couple of trips to and from an adjunct teaching job, I dub this "The Road to Nowhere." Since the road leads to the expressway, it arguably goes *somewhere*, physically, I suppose. But not in any other way.

I once read that a cause of depression is boredom, that people suffering from it require more sensory stimulation.

Maybe that's why canaries learn a new song every spring. They won't get depressed. As if having bright plumage and the ability to fly aren't enough.

If only I were a canary, if only I learned a new song whenever I entered The Road to Nowhere. But I am depressed, and morose people don't feel like singing. Or even if they sing, it's the same old dirge over and over.

Therefore, my main means of escaping boredom and depression—before I even enter The Road to Nowhere—is to swing through the car wash. Here, my Toyota RAV glides into a swirl of red and blue felt pads. Neon-colored pink, yellow, and green soap bubbles cascade across the windows. I float as if through a mystical underground cavern sequestered from the outside world.

Sure, the trips through the car wash are for entertainment. They're also calming, secluded, before I descend into my personal version of hell. Ironically, since the tires aren't moving, I still feel more alive than while actually driving The Road to Nowhere.

With my hands in my lap, not steering, it's as if some cosmic force controls movement and direction. My car scrolls through the underbody flush and rust inhibitors, the clear-coat sealer. The brush hub cleans the lower parts of the chassis. Then the car sails on to pressure nozzles and silicone tire jets. Sprays of water billow with me cocooned, as if suspended, in a special blend of amniotic fluid muting the outside world. This not only engages me, but in a moment of magical thinking, I pretend it will protect the car *and* me well into the next millennium.

Upon entering The Road to Nowhere, I pretend I'm still in the wet-womb protection of the car wash. Only then, I no longer see the houses, the farms, the excruciating isolation.

If only The Road to Nowhere were one expansive carnival-ride car wash. But here I am, slogging along in its endlessness, memories of the car wash fading. I'm unable to relax into the pastoral, the nothingness of it all. It's like entering what I fear might be the Afterlife. *My* Afterlife. As if I possess enough consciousness to know the road might never end but not enough energy to actually end it. Seek an off-ramp. An exit. Instead, I'm trapped, like Death: one long endless road to nowhere.

With no canaries accompanying the journey.

Sometimes I wonder what would happen in the car wash if I put the transmission into drive. Could the rainbow bubbles, the dreamy

Seeking Paradise

steam, the tunnel with flashing lights spew me forward to live in a constant glowing cataract of water?

What would happen if I slid the car into reverse? Would the tunnel cast me backward whereby I'd have decades to undo or re-do all the calamities, catastrophes, confusions, chaos, and misdemeanors?

Or should the car remain in neutral, in limbo, with nothing distressing to distract or upset this state of euphoria?

Is the road a symbol? The car wash? Why does one devastate while the other reassures?

Has my whole life existed on *A* Road to Nowhere? I traveled this metaphoric road with Forrest, the older man who lived across the street from my college dorm. That relationship stalled in the breakdown lane before it even began. I peregrinated it with Rick, the paleontologist who drove his Jeep to bat caves, who sped us to the woods one night when we were caught by his wife. I also hit The Metaphoric Road to Nowhere with the physics professor and his indented forehead, who traded sex for a passing grade while the antimatter of his melanoma metastasized through his soul. My soul? After all, I drove *My* Road to Nowhere with an ice-coated windshield, blind spots of denial, a cracked rearview mirror—never seeing how the past, rutted and ruined, *repeated, repeated, repeated.*

Am I drawn to the car wash as if it represents hope? Do I think the car wash will cleanse the past?

Would I need an eternity in a car wash to rinse all the dusty residue off the skin of my past?

The RAV cruises into the rinse cycle, waterdrops so soft they sound like inhaling, or a gentle spring rain. Steam billows. I can't see out the rearview mirror. I don't need to. I know where I've been. But where am I going? Will I know once my car shoots out the end of this tunnel? Is a new destination possible? Can I finally just *be*?

Literally, I travel The Road to Nowhere on Tuesdays to teach. When, eventually, I reach campus I park and enter an almost-deserted building housing the English department. I climb stairs to the classroom, passing no one, the soles of my shoes echoing *click-clicks*. I never see other teachers. No one greets or welcomes me to the department. For two hours, late afternoon into evening, my twelve students and I huddle in what seems like the only lit classroom in the building.

Then, finally, the semester ends. Thank God.

I don't want to drive The Road to Nowhere ever again. Not literally. Not metaphorically. Because even if I never reach that paradisial land of snow leopards and eternal car washes, I still write it. Imagine it. I point myself in its direction and drive, hyacinth petal to metal, beyond the beyond.

ACKNOWLEDGMENTS

Profound thanks and deep gratitude to Courtney Ochsner, Sara Springsteen, Tish Fobben, Rosemary Sekora, Sarah Kee, Lindsey Welch, and the University of Nebraska Press for its continued support of my writing.

Many thanks to the following journals and presses for publishing these individual essays, some with different titles or in different versions.

"At the Apollo Theatre," *Sweet: A Literary Confection* 15 (September 5, 2022).

"Coming Attractions," *Under the Gum Tree*, Winter 2023.

"Time Travel for Beginners," *Paddle Shots: A River Pretty Anthology* 3 (Spring 2023).

"Harbor Lights," *Acetylene Torch Songs: Writing True Stories to Ignite the Soul* (University of Nebraska Press, 2024).

"7-Up as a Cure for Irony," *Maine Review* 8, no. 2 (May 20, 2022).

"Library with Hyacinth, Girl, and Guns," *Short Reads*, no. 010 (May 31, 2023).

"How to Find a Snow Leopard in Georgia," *Dillydoun Review* 16 (May 2022).

"The Poetic Sentence," *Chautauqua* 20, no. 1 (2022); reprinted by permission of *Chautauqua*, copyright 2022.

"On Liminality," *Slag Glass City*, October 2022.

"Remembrance of Things Past," *Sweet: A Literary Confection* 15 (September 5, 2022).

"The Long Road Out of Eden," *In Short Journal*, May 2025.

"The Soft Beauty of an Ordinary Life," *Dorothy Parker's Ashes*, January 4, 2024.

"Trashy," *The Ravens Perch*, February 27, 2023.

"Degas Paints the Chippendales and Me," *The Pinch Journal* 44, no. 1 (Spring 2024).

"The Origin of Her Superpowers," *Becoming Real: Women Reclaim the Power of the Imagined through Speculative Nonfiction* (Regal Press, 2024).

"A Grand Unified Theory of Disease," *Jabberwock Review*, Summer/Fall 2024.

"The Memory Box," *Essay* 23 (Spring 2023).

Also by Sue William Silverman

CREATIVE NONFICTION

Because I Remember Terror, Father, I Remember You
(Winner of the Association of Writers and Writing Programs Award Series)

Love Sick: One Woman's Journey through Sexual Addiction
(Also an Original Lifetime TV Movie)

The Pat Boone Fan Club: My Life as a White Anglo-Saxon Jew

How to Survive Death and Other Inconveniences
(*Foreword Reviews* Indie Book of the Year Award, Gold Star 2021 Clara Johnson Award for Women's Literature, sponsored by Jane's Stories Press Foundation)

INSTRUCTIONAL

Fearless Confessions: A Writer's Guide to Memoir

Acetylene Torch Songs: Writing True Stories to Ignite the Soul
(Silver Medal: Independent Publishing Book Awards)

POETRY

Hieroglyphics in Neon

If the Girl Never Learns

Crayon Colors for Serial Killers